STECK-VAUGHN

Target
SPELLING 780

W9-DCW-812

Margaret Scarborough
Mary F. Brigham
Teresa A. Miller

STECK-VAUGHN
ELEMENTARY · SECONDARY · ADULT · LIBRARY

A Harcourt Company

www.steck-vaughn.com

Table of Contents

Acknowledgments

Editorial Director:	Stephanie Muller
Editor:	Kathleen Gower Wiseman
Associate Director of Design:	Cynthia Ellis
Design Managers:	Sheryl Cota, Katie Nott
Illustrators:	Peg Dougherty, Jimmy Longacre, Cindy Aarvig, David Griffin, Lynn McClain
Cover Design:	Bassett & Brush Design, Todd Disrud and Stephanie Schreiber

ISBN 0-7398-2459-7

2 3 4 5 6 7 8 9 DBH 04 03 02 01

Word Study Plan

1 **LOOK** at the word. _____

2 **SAY** the word. _____

3 **THINK** about each letter. _____

4 **SPELL** the word aloud. _____

5 **WRITE** the word. _____

6 **CHECK** the spelling. _____

7 **REPEAT** the steps
if you need more practice. _____

Name _____

1

Spelling Strategies

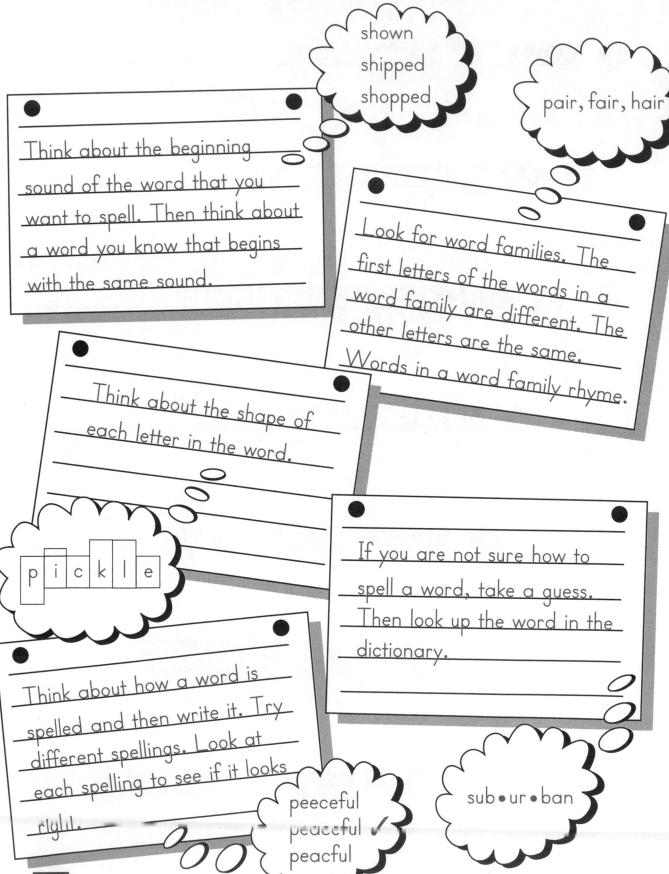

DAY 1

Words with *er*

her	jerk	perch	herd
fern	nerve	verb	perk

A **Fill in each blank with a spelling word.**

1. She felt sick, so I took _____ some soup.

2. A _____ is a nice plant to grow.

3. It takes _____ to be a firefighter.

4. The bird is resting on its _____.

5. The carnival ride made me _____ from side to side.

6. An action word is called a _____.

7. The coffee is about to _____.

8. A _____ of wild horses ran through the field.

B **Circle the word that is the same as the top one.**

her	fern	jerk	nerve	perch	verb	herd	perk
him	fenn	jerk	rerve	porch	werb	berd	perk
hen	fenr	jark	nirve	perch	verd	herd	pork
yer	fern	jarh	narve	qerch	verb	herb	park
(her)	farn	yerk	nerve	pench	vorb	harb	qerk

C **Write a spelling word under each picture.**

1. _____   2. _____   3. _____

Name _____

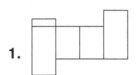

Words with *er*

her	jerk	perch	herd
fern	nerve	verb	perk

A Fill in the boxes with the correct spelling words.

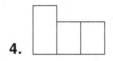 1.

2.

3.

4.

5.

6.

B Write the spelling word that rhymes with the word pair.

1. turn   learn   _____

2. curve   swerve   _____

3. lurk   perk   _____

4. bird   word   _____

C Write each spelling word beside its clue.

fern   **1.** a plant that likes wet places

_____ **2.** courage

_____ **3.** goes with "she"

_____ **4.** a pole or rod for a bird to rest on

_____ **5.** many animals in a group

_____ **6.** to become lively

_____ **7.** a quick, sharp pull or twist

_____ **8.** a word that shows action

Words with *er*

her	jerk	perch	herd
fern	nerve	verb	perk

A Find the missing letters. Then write the word.

1. v ___ ___ b   _____

2. n ___ r v ___   _____

B Write the spelling words in alphabetical (ABC) order.

1. _____   2. _____   3. _____   4. _____

5. _____   6. _____   7. _____   8. _____

C Use the correct spelling words to complete the story.

The cowboys who went on trail drives years ago are the real heroes of the West. They would move a _____ of cattle from the South to the North. Most cattle trails ended in Kansas. There the beef from the herd was sent east by train.

Trail drives were full of danger and lasted for months. The weather wasn't always good, and thieves would try to steal herds. At night, one cowboy would _____ on his horse to watch for thieves while the other cowboys slept.

It took _____ to be a cowboy on trail drives.

D Complete each sentence.

1. It's <u>her</u> turn to _____.

2. The <u>fern</u> I bought is _____.

Name _____

DAY 4

Words with *er*

her	jerk	perch	herd
fern	nerve	verb	perk

A **Fill in each blank with a spelling word.**

1. Write the words that begin with *per*.

_____   _____

2. Write the words that begin with *h*.

_____   _____

3. Write the word that ends with a vowel. _____

B **Use the correct spelling words to answer these riddles.**

1. This is a sharp pull, push, or bounce.

What is it? _____

2. This is the courage you need to take a test. It also names a type of fiber in your body.

What is it? _____

3. Birds like to rest on this. It can also be a kind of fish.

What is it? _____

C **Use each spelling word in a sentence.**

herd   _____

nerve   _____

perk   _____

fern   _____

verb   _____

Words with *ur*

turn	purse	burst	church
burn	nurse	curve	curb

A **Fill in each blank with a spelling word.**

1. The wedding was held in the _____.

2. The _____ in the hospital was very nice to me.

3. It's my _____ to do the dishes.

4. The balloon _____ from too much air.

5. When a line bends, it's called a _____.

6. Don't _____ your hand on the hot stove!

7. We stood on the _____ before crossing the street.

8. Do you have a pen in your _____?

B **Circle the letters that are the same in all the spelling words.**

burst   turn   burn   nurse   church   curve   purse   curb

C **Write the spelling words that rhyme with the word pair.**

1. first   thirst   _____

2. fern   churn   _____

3. verse   worse   _____

4. search   perch   _____

5. herb   verb   _____

D **Complete the sentence.**

The balloon <u>burst</u> _____.

Name _____

Lesson 2

Words with *ur*

turn	purse	burst	church
burn	nurse	curve	curb

DAY 2

A **Circle the word that is the same as the top one.**

burst	turn	burn	nurse	church	curve	purse	curb
burst	tunn	durn	nnrse	church	carve	qurse	carb
bursh	tunr	burn	nurse	cburch	cnrve	porse	curd
burts	furn	barn	narse	charch	curve	parse	curb
burns	turn	bunn	nunse	chorch	corve	purse	cunb

B **Answer the questions with spelling words.**

1. Which word means "to explode or break open"? _____

2. Which word means "a small bag or pouch"? _____

3. Which word means "the edge of a street"? _____

4. Which word means "to be on fire"? _____

5. Which word means "a bending line"? _____

C **Fill in the boxes with the correct spelling words.**

1.

2.

3.

4.

5.

6.

D **Find the missing letters. Then write the word.**

1. c h ___ ___ ___ ___   _____

2. p ___ ___ s e   _____

8

DAY
3

Words with *ur*

turn	purse	burst	church
burn	nurse	curve	curb

A **Use spelling words in two sentences.**

1. _____

2. _____

B **Use the correct spelling words to complete the story.**

I will never forget the first time I rode with my brother in his car. He was the

best driver I had ever seen.

He had just bought a new car, and he wanted to take me for a drive. My

brother never forgot to signal before he was about to _____ a corner.

He stopped at the stop light near the old, stone _____. If a street

began to _____, he gently stepped on the brakes. And when he pulled

up next to the _____, he didn't even bump it! Someday I hope that I

will drive as well as my brother.

C **Write the spelling words in alphabetical order.**

1. _____   2. _____   3. _____   4. _____

5. _____   6. _____   7. _____   8. _____

D **Write the spelling words that have five letters.**

_____   _____

_____   _____

Name _____

Lesson 2

Words with *ur*

turn	purse	burst	church
burn	nurse	curve	curb

A One word is wrong in each sentence. Circle the wrong word. Then fill in the blank with a spelling word that makes sense.

1. The clown gave me a shot in my arm. _____

2. The balloon cried from having too much air. _____

3. You light a candle so that it will walk. _____

4. She keeps her wallet in her garden. _____

B Write a spelling word under each picture.

1. _____   2. _____   3. _____

C Answer the questions with spelling words.

1. Which word begins and ends with the same sound?

_____

2. Which words end with silent *e*?

_____   _____   _____

3. Which words have the letter *b* in them?

_____   _____   _____

4. Which words end in *urn*?

_____   _____

10

DAY 1

Words with *au*

launch	vault	fault	haunt
gauze	haul	cause	August

A **Fill in each blank with a spelling word.**

1. Please put my money in the bank's _____.

2. We need to _____ away all of the empty boxes.

3. It's my _____ that we were late.

4. The space center will _____ a new rocket.

5. What was the _____ of the fire?

6. You wrap a burn in a _____ bandage.

7. The story says that a noisy ghost may _____ the old house.

8. _____ is the eighth month of the year.

B **Find the missing letters. Then write the word.**

1. v ___ ___ l t   _____

2. ___ ___ g u s t   _____

C **Circle the letters that are the same in all the spelling words.**

launch   gauze   vault   haul   fault   cause   haunt   August

D **Write the spelling words in alphabetical order.**

1. _____   2. _____   3. _____   4. _____

5. _____   6. _____   7. _____   8. _____

Name _____

DAY 2

Words with *au*

launch	vault	fault	haunt
gauze	haul	cause	August

A **Use the correct spelling words to complete the story.**

Have you ever seen the _____ of a rocket? We saw one

launched last _____. It was the best part of my summer. If you

think a rocket looks big on TV, you should see the real thing!

It takes a few days just to _____ a rocket to the launch pad.

When it takes off, the power and noise _____ the ground to rumble

and shake.

B **Write each spelling word beside its clue.**

_____   **1.** to send off or set in motion

_____   **2.** to disturb

_____   **3.** a room in a bank

_____   **4.** a piece of cloth used in first aid

_____   **5.** the name of a month

_____   **6.** blame

_____   **7.** to carry

_____   **8.** something that brings about a result

C **Write the spelling words that name things you <u>cannot</u> touch.**

1. _____   **2.** _____   **3.** _____

4. _____   **5.** _____   **0.** _____

DAY
3

Words with *au*

launch	vault	fault	haunt
gauze	haul	cause	August

A Circle the word that is the same as the top one.

launch	gauze	vault	haul	fault	cause	haunt	August
luanch	gouze	vault	baul	tault	couse	haunt	Aagust
lauuch	gauze	vaulf	hual	faulf	cause	baunt	Augusf
launch	pauze	voult	haul	fualt	cauze	haunf	August
leunch	guaze	wault	houl	fault	cuase	hount	Aujust

B Write the spelling words that rhyme with the word pair.

1. laws   saws   _____

2. fall   call   _____

3. malt   salt   _____

4. want   jaunt   _____

C Use each spelling word in a sentence.

launch _____

gauze _____

vault _____

haul _____

fault _____

cause _____

haunt _____

August _____

Name _____

Words with *au*

launch	vault	fault	haunt
gauze	haul	cause	August

A Find each hidden word from the list.

launch	vault	fault	haunt
gauze	haul	cause	August
law	draw	how	plow

u	r	l	a	u	n	c	h	m	y	l	b	e	s	t	h	f
r	i	e	u	n	d	w	h	y	d	a	o	n	d	r	a	w
t	w	v	g	a	u	z	e	h	o	w	e	g	o	o	u	t
t	f	a	u	l	t	o	s	a	w	i	m	o	r	g	l	o
f	o	u	s	r	a	c	a	u	r	r	i	d	e	i	n	y
o	u	l	t	r	n	e	w	n	l	i	t	p	l	o	w	t
l	e	t	s	p	o	r	t	t	s	c	a	u	s	e	c	o
u	l	d	h	a	v	e	a	l	o	t	o	f	f	u	n	i

B Answer the questions with spelling words.

1. Which word begins with a capital letter? _____

2. Which words end with a silent *e*?

   _____   _____

3. Which words begin with the same first letter?

   _____   _____

4. Which words end with *ult*?

   _____   _____

5. Which word ends with *ch*?

   _____

Homonyms

red	not	maid	be
read	knot	made	bee

A **Fill in each blank with a spelling word.**

1. I _____ about you in the newspaper.

2. Can you tie a _____ in the rope?

3. The _____ will clean up the hotel room.

4. She _____ me a great birthday cake.

5. I am _____ going to the party on Friday.

6. When the light turns _____, you have to stop.

7. Will you _____ my valentine?

8. A _____ stung me on my foot!

B **Find the missing letters. Then write the word.**

1. m __ __ d   _____

2. m __ __ e   _____

3. r __ __ d   _____

4. __ __ __ t   _____

C **Write a spelling word under each picture.**

1. _____   2. _____   3. _____

Name _____

15

Lesson 4   Homonyms

DAY 2

red	not	maid	be
read	knot	made	bee

A Fill in the boxes with the correct spelling words.

1.
2.
3.
4.
5.
6.
7.
8.

B Write each spelling word beside its clue.

_____ 1. what you do with a book

_____ 2. caused something to be or to happen

_____ 3. something tied together, or a tangle

_____ 4. traffic light color that means "stop"

_____ 5. an insect that makes honey

_____ 6. the homonym for "made"

C Use the correct spelling words to complete the story.

My aunt was hanging out clothes on the line, when a _____

stung her.

"Ouch!" she cried. She ran inside, holding her arm. The bee's sting

_____ a big purple and _____ knot.

She found a first-aid book and _____ that you should try to

_____ calm, remove the stinger, and put medicine on the knot. After

my aunt did that, she felt much better.

16

Homonyms

red	not	maid	be
read	knot	made	bee

A **Fill in each blank with a spelling word.**

1. Write the words that end with *d*.

_____   _____   _____

2. Write the word that ends with two *e*'s. _____

3. Write the words that have the letter *o*.

_____   _____

B **Write the spelling words that rhyme with the word pair.**

1. paid   raid   _____

2. lot   cot   _____

3. see   me   _____

4. fed   bed   _____

C **Use each spelling word in a sentence.**

red   _____

read   _____

not   _____

knot   _____

maid   _____

made   _____

be   _____

bee   _____

Name _____

Homonyms

red	not	maid	be
read	knot	made	bee

A Find each hidden word from the list.

red	not	maid	be
read	knot	made	bee
oil	spoil	coin	join

```
i  l  l  n  i  t  r  a  i  n  o  r  b  e  e  w  i  l
i  s  p  o  i  l  t  s  o  n  o  w  o  r  c  i  s  i
g  o  i  t  n  g  t  o  i  d  o  a  n  j  o  i  n  y
h  i  n  g  d  i  f  f  l  e  m  r  e  n  i  t  t  o
b  e  a  y  c  a  n  i  h  e  a  l  p  y  n  o  u  w
t  h  y  r  e  a  d  o  u  r  i  b  a  g  g  a  g  e
w  o  u  e  l  d  l  o  v  e  d  t  o  h  a  v  e  a
i  g  t  d  i  p  w  h  e  n  c  a  k  n  o  t  n  y
u  c  o  m  e  o  m  a  d  e  v  e  r  t  o  s  e  e
e  w  w  c  a  n  h  a  v  e  l  o  t  s  o  f  f  u
```

B Write the spelling words in alphabetical order.

1. _____ 2. _____ 3. _____ 4. _____

5. _____ 6. _____ 7. _____ 8. _____

C Fill in each blank with a spelling word.

1. Write the word that names a color. _____

2. Write the word that starts with a silent letter. _____

3. Write the word that names a flying insect. _____

4. Write the word that has only two letters. _____

Lesson 5

Words with *aw*

crawl	dawn	fawn	flaw
lawn	yawn	claw	straw

A **Fill in each blank with a spelling word.**

1. Yesterday we saw a mother deer and her _____ in the woods behind our house.

2. People _____ when they are tired.

3. Will you help me mow the _____?

4. My brother wakes up at the crack of _____.

5. I had to _____ under the table to find my glasses.

6. A mistake in something is called a _____.

7. My new hat is made out of _____.

8. The cat's _____ is very sharp.

B **Write the spelling words that end in *aw*.**

_____   _____   _____

C **Fill in the boxes with the correct spelling words.**

1. 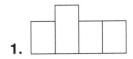   2. 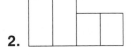   3.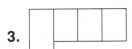

4.   5.    6.

7. 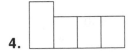   8.

Name _____

Words with *aw*

crawl	dawn	fawn	flaw
lawn	yawn	claw	straw

A Circle the word that is the same as the top one.

crawl	lawn	dawn	yawn	fawn	claw	flaw	straw
craml	lown	bawn	yawn	famn	clow	flow	strow
crawl	lamn	dawn	gawn	bawn	claw	flam	sfraw
cnawl	lawn	down	yown	fawn	clam	falw	straw
crowl	lewn	bamn	yawr	fown	clau	flaw	srtaw

B Write the spelling words in alphabetical order.

1. _____ 2. _____ 3. _____ 4. _____

5. _____ 6. _____ 7. _____ 8. _____

C Write each spelling word beside its clue.

_____ 1. a thin tube to drink through

_____ 2. what babies do before they walk

_____ 3. a baby deer

_____ 4. what people do when they are tired

_____ 5. the first light of the morning

_____ 6. a mistake

_____ 7. a sharp nail on a cat's paw

_____ 8. the part of a yard that is usually mowed

Lesson 5

DAY 3

Words with *aw*

crawl	dawn	fawn	flaw
lawn	yawn	claw	straw

A Find the missing letters. Then write the word.

1. c r __ __ __ _____

2. s t __ __ __ _____

B Write a spelling word under each picture.

1. _____ 2. _____ 3. _____

C Write the spelling words that rhyme with the word pair.

1. lawn   yawn   _____

2. flaw   straw   _____

3. drawl   brawl   _____

D Circle the letters that are the same in all the spelling words.

crawl   lawn   dawn   yawn   fawn   claw   flaw   straw

E Complete each sentence.

1. We had to <u>crawl</u> _____.

2. I woke up at <u>dawn</u> and _____.

3. He found a <u>flaw</u> in _____.

Name _____

DAY 4

Words with *aw*

crawl	dawn	fawn	flaw
lawn	yawn	claw	straw

A **Use the correct spelling words to complete the story.**

I awoke at _____ to a chorus of terrible sounds. I heard

hissing and spitting and growling. Two cats were having a fight outside.

I had never heard such a racket before! I jumped out of bed and ran

downstairs.

I grabbed a broom made of _____ and went outside to stop the

fight. The cats were on my front _____. They turned to look at me.

Then one cat tried to _____ the other. I shouted, "Stop!" Both cats

sped out of my yard.

I saw one _____ under a house. The other cat ran down the street.

What a way to start the day!

B **Use each spelling word in a sentence.**

crawl _____

lawn _____

dawn _____

yawn _____

fawn _____

claw _____

flaw _____

straw _____

her	perch	burst	church	launch
fern	verb	turn	curve	gauze
jerk	herd	burn	purse	vault
nerve	perk	nurse	curb	haul

A **Write a spelling word under each picture.**

1. _____ 2. _____ 3. _____

B **Fill in each blank with a spelling word.**

1. The bird sat on its _____.

2. Buffaloes run in a _____.

3. The balloon had too much air and _____.

4. The car slowed down around the _____.

5. _____ new hat is very pretty.

6. When I get sick, I call my friend who is a _____.

7. Did you _____ away the trash?

8. They will _____ the rocket tomorrow.

9. Please _____ left at the light.

10. The bank puts the money in the _____.

11. Can you find the noun and the _____ in that sentence?

12. I will put a piece of _____ over the scrape.

Name _____

fault	red	maid	crawl	fawn
cause	read	made	lawn	claw
haunt	not	be	dawn	flaw
August	knot	bee	yawn	straw

C **Write the spelling words that rhyme with the word pair.**

1. law   flaw   _____

2. free   tree   _____

3. hot   rot   _____

4. saws   pause   _____

5. lawn   dawn   _____

D **Use the correct spelling words to complete the story.**

Last year I went to visit my friend. It was in the month of _____.

One night my friend told me a story about a haunted house. She had _____

the story in a book.

The story said that there was a strange house on a hill. The neighbors that

lived near the house always heard loud noises coming from it. When they went to

see what was making the loud noises, no one would be there. They also saw

lights flashing on and off in the house. Sometimes they would see a blue or

_____ light that was shining on the porch. This always _____

them feel funny. The noises would last all night long and then stop at

_____. They never did find out what it was that made the loud noises. If

I had lived near that house, I don't think I would even want to know!

DAY 1

Words with *oo*

foot	wood	stood	crook
hook	brook	hood	cook

A Fill in each blank with a spelling word.

1. The water in the little _____ was cold.

2. Let's bring some _____ in for the fire.

3. You have to put bait on the _____ to catch a fish.

4. I _____ up to see my friend score the goal.

5. The _____ of a car covers the engine.

6. He fell down and broke his _____.

7. The _____ did not burn the food.

8. The curved part of an umbrella handle is called a _____.

B Find the missing letters. Then write the word.

1. s t ___ ___ d   _____

2. c ___ ___ ___ k   _____

C Circle the letters that are the same in all the spelling words.

foot   hook   wood   brook   stood   hood   crook   cook

D One word is wrong in each sentence. Circle the wrong word. Then fill in the blank with a spelling word that makes sense.

1. I caught the fish on a toothpick.   _____

2. We need water to make the fire burn.   _____

3. You should thank the plate for the food we ate.   _____

4. We all flew up when our team scored.   _____

Name _____

Words with *oo*

| foot | wood | stood | crook |
| hook | brook | hood | cook |

A Circle the word that is the same as the top one.

foot	hook	wood	brook	stood	hood	crook	cook
foof	book	mood	bnook	sfood	hood	cnook	dook
feet	hook	woob	breek	stood	heed	crook	beek
toof	heek	wood	drook	stoob	hoob	creek	booh
foot	hooh	weed	brook	steed	bood	croak	cook

B Write the spelling words that rhyme with the word pair.

1. hook   crook   _____

2. soot   put   _____

3. hood   stood   _____

4. brook   cook   _____

5. wood   hood   _____

C Write the spelling words that name things you can touch.

1. _____   2. _____   3. _____

4. _____   5. _____   6. _____

7. _____

D Write the spelling words in alphabetical order.

1. _____   2. _____   3. _____   4. _____

5. _____   6. _____   7. _____   8. _____

Lesson 6 **Words with *oo***

foot	wood	stood	crook
hook	brook	hood	cook

A **Use the correct spelling words to complete the story.**

I went fishing last week with my friend. We _____ beside a little

_____ to catch the fish. We were going to _____ what we

caught.

I cast out my line and caught a big fish. I was pulling the _____

out of the fish's mouth when my _____ slipped. The fish flew out of

my hand and into the water. There went our supper!

B **Write a spelling word under each picture.**

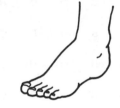   

1. _____ 2. _____ 3. _____

C **Fill in each blank with a spelling word.**

1. Write the words that end with *ook*.

_____   _____

_____   _____

2. Write the words that end with *ood*.

_____   _____   _____

3. Write the word that ends with a *t*.

_____

Name _____

Words with *oo*

foot	wood	stood	crook
hook	brook	hood	cook

A **Find each hidden word from the list.**

foot	brook	crook	proud
hook	stood	cook	ground
wood	hood	cloud	pound

```
l  e  t  s  g  o  p  f  l  y  a  k  i  t  e  u  p  w
h  e  f  r  e  t  o  h  h  e  a  i  w  o  o  d  r  i
s  l  o  i  p  g  u  h  o  t  o  h  l  e  t  s  g  c
o  f  o  l  r  y  n  a  o  k  i  t  b  e  w  h  a  o
t  a  t  w  o  o  d  n  k  d  e  r  r  f  u  l  p  o
e  r  s  o  u  n  b  a  r  b  s  t  o  o  d  a  r  k
a  i  s  s  d  h  h  e  i  s  k  i  o  n  d  a  n  d
u  n  d  e  r  s  o  t  c  r  o  o  k  a  n  d  i  n
g  a  n  d  i  w  o  a  g  r  o  u  n  d  n  t  m  y
c  h  c  l  o  u  d  i  l  d  r  e  n  t  o  b  e  l
```

B **Use each spelling word in a sentence.**

hook _____

wood _____

brook _____

C **Change one letter in each spelling word to make a new word.**

_____ **1.** Change "brook" to something you read.

_____ **2.** Change "foot" to what an owl says.

_____ **3.** Change "hook" to the name of a person who fixes food.

Words with *oo*

food	bloom	booth	goose
noon	loose	tooth	proof

A **Fill in each blank with a spelling word.**

1. The flowers are ready to _____.

2. I am calling you from a phone _____.

3. I need a belt because my pants are too _____.

4. The _____ he cooks is really great!

5. The dentist fixed her _____.

6. Let's eat lunch today at 12 _____.

7. There is _____ that Earth is round.

8. A _____ looks like a big duck.

B **Circle the letters that are the same in all the spelling words.**

food   noon   bloom   loose   booth   tooth   goose   proof

C **Use the correct spelling words to complete the story.**

I sold flowers at our county fair. I rented a _____ and set up a

sign. At _____ the crowds arrived. Most of the other booths sold

_____.

A _____ in the booth next to mine got _____ and ate

some of my flowers. Then somebody bought the goose. I sold a lot of

flowers, but I used most of my money to buy food at the fair.

Name _____

Words with *oo*

| food | bloom | booth | goose |
| noon | loose | tooth | proof |

A Circle the word that is the same as the top one.

food	noon	bloom	loose	booth	tooth	goose	proof
foob	gnoo	dloom	loose	booht	booth	goose	groof
feed	nune	bloow	leese	dooth	tooth	joose	proot
tood	noon	bloom	loase	booth	footh	geese	proof
food	soon	bleem	looes	beeth	thoot	gooes	pnoof

B Write the spelling words in alphabetical order.

1. _____ 2. _____ 3. _____ 4. _____

5. _____ 6. _____ 7. _____ 8. _____

C Write each spelling word beside its clue.

_____ **1.** an animal that makes a honking sound

_____ **2.** what we eat to stay alive

_____ **3.** the place where people vote

_____ **4.** one of the things you chew with

_____ **5.** lunchtime

_____ **6.** the flower on a plant

_____ **7.** what you use to prove something

_____ **8.** not tight

Lesson 7   Words with *oo*

food	bloom	booth	goose
noon	loose	tooth	proof

A **Find the missing letters. Then write the word.**

1. ___ ___ o n   _____

2. b l ___ ___ ___   _____

B **Use spelling words to complete the puzzle.**

Across

2. Flowers ___ in spring.

4. The boy lost his first ___.

6. not tight

7. what we eat

Down

1. lunchtime

2. a stall at a fair

3. It looks like a duck.

5. evidence

Name _____

DAY
4

Words with *oo*

food	bloom	booth	goose
noon	loose	tooth	proof

A Fill in the boxes with the correct spelling words.

1.

2.

3.

4.

5.

6.

7.

8.

B Write a spelling word under each picture.

1. _____   2. _____   3. _____

C Use each spelling word in a sentence.

food _____

noon _____

bloom _____

loose _____

booth _____

tooth _____

goose _____

proof _____

32

DAY 1

Words with *ie*

| thief | niece | field | brief |
| chief | piece | shield | yield |

A **Fill in each blank with a spelling word.**

1. Who is the _____ of police?

2. Your brother's daughter is your _____.

3. An umbrella will _____ you from the rain.

4. A farmer plants crops in a _____.

5. I would love a _____ of cake.

6. The _____ ran off with my purse.

7. The yellow, three-sided road sign means to _____.

8. She told us a _____ story, and then we left early.

B **Write the spelling word that rhymes with the word pair.**

1. shield   yield   _____

2. chief   brief   _____

3. geese   piece   _____

C **Write the spelling words that name things you can touch.**

1. _____   2. _____   3. _____

4. _____   5. _____   6. _____

D **Complete each sentence.**

1. I saw a <u>field</u> of _____.

2. May I have a <u>piece</u> of _____?

Name _____

DAY 2

Words with *ie*

thief	niece	field	brief
chief	piece	shield	yield

A Find the missing letters. Then write the word.

1. s ___ ___ ___ l ___   _____

2. y ___ ___ ___ d   _____

3. t ___ i ___ ___   _____

B Write each spelling word beside its clue.

_____   **1.** an open land area often used for planting crops

_____   **2.** the leader of a group or tribe

_____   **3.** a sign that means slow down and let others go first

_____   **4.** a person who steals

_____   **5.** your sister's daughter

_____   **6.** a part or a bit of something

_____   **7.** something that is short or doesn't take much time

_____   **8.** something that protects you

C Circle the letters that are the same in all the spelling words.

thief   chief   niece   piece   field   shield   brief   yield

Lesson 8 — Words with *ie*

DAY 3

thief	niece	field	brief
chief	piece	shield	yield

A Fill in the boxes with the correct spelling words.

1.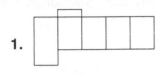

2.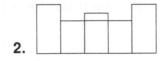

3.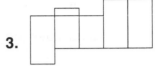

4.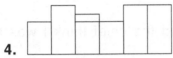

5.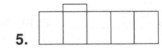

6.

B One word is wrong in each sentence. Circle the wrong word. Then fill in the blank with a spelling word that makes sense.

1. I planted corn in the toaster, and it grew very well. _____

2. My brother's little girl is my aunt. _____

3. The police chased the chair down the street. _____

4. Each person got a bucket of cake at the party. _____

5. The knights in the castle had a feather to protect them from flying arrows. _____

6. When you see the word "store," you must slow down and let others go first. _____

7. The leader of a company is sometimes called its flower. _____

8. If you want people to listen to your speech, it should be boring and to the point. _____

C Write the spelling words that end with a silent letter.

_____   _____

Name _____

DAY 4

Words with *ie*

thief	niece	field	brief
chief	piece	shield	yield

A **Use the correct spelling words to complete the story.**

My _____ and I were out for a ride in my car. Suddenly, I saw

lights flash behind me. The _____ of police made us stop by the

side of the road.

Did I run through a _____ sign, or did the chief think I was a

_____? I was afraid I would get a ticket and have to pay a fine.

But the chief was very nice. He said a _____ of my taillight was

broken. I thanked him and went on my way.

B **Write the spelling words in alphabetical order.**

1. _____   2. _____   3. _____   4. _____

5. _____   6. _____   7. _____   8. _____

C **Use each spelling word in a sentence.**

niece _____

field _____

brief _____

yield _____

shield _____

piece _____

chief _____

thief _____

Lesson 9   Homonyms

DAY 1

road	pail	ate	see
rode	pale	eight	sea

A   **Fill in each blank with a spelling word.**

1. A _____ is a bucket in which you carry water.

2. _____ the horse running down the street!

3. You look as _____ as a ghost.

4. We stopped for a picnic on the side of the _____.

5. They _____ horses all day at the ranch.

6. We _____ too much watermelon at the party.

7. The huge aquarium had many _____ animals.

8. _____ people is too many to fit into a car.

B   **Circle the correct answer to complete the sentence.**

1. "Pail" and "pale" have different meanings, but they _____.

     sound the same   look the same   feel the same

2. Words that sound the same but are not spelled the same are _____.

     synonyms   homonyms   antonyms

3. The words in this lesson are called _____.

     synonyms   homonyms   antonyms

4. It is _____ that this lesson has four homonym pairs.

     true   false

C   **Find the missing letters. Then write the word.**

1. p a ___ e   _____

2. e i ___ ___ ___   _____

Name _____

Lesson 9 Homonyms

road	pail	ate	see
rode	pale	eight	sea

A Write the spelling words that rhyme with the word pair.

1. load   toad   _____

2. sail   tail   _____

3. date   bait   _____

4. be   fee   _____

5. fail   sail   _____

6. sewed   code   _____

7. rate   late   _____

B Write a spelling word under each picture.

1. _____   **2.** _____   **3.** _____

C Write the spelling words in alphabetical order.

1. _____ **2.** _____ **3.** _____ **4.** _____

5. _____ **6.** _____ **7.** _____ **8.** _____

D Write the spelling words that name things you can touch.

1. _____   **2.** _____   **3.** _____

38

Lesson 9   Homonyms

road	pail	ate	see
rode	pale	eight	sea

A   **Use the correct spelling words to complete the story.**

My friends and I spent a week by the _____. We had a contest

to _____ who could build the best sand castle. We decided to start

at _____ o'clock in the morning.

On the day of the contest, I woke up early. I _____ breakfast

and found a _____ to put the sand in. I _____ my bike down

to the shore.

We started building castles. By ten o'clock, we were finished. I had worked

hard on my castle, and I was very tired. The sun was already turning my

_____ face red.

I felt much better after the judges voted and named the winner. My sand

castle won first prize!

B   **Write each spelling word beside its clue.**

_____   **1.** the number after seven

_____   **2.** the ocean

_____   **3.** what you do with your eyes

_____   **4.** not having much color

_____   **5.** a bucket for carrying water

_____   **6.** what cars travel on

Name _____

Homonyms

| road | pail | ate | see |
| rode | pale | eight | sea |

A **Fill in the boxes with the correct spelling words.**

1.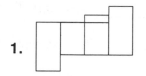

2.

3.

4.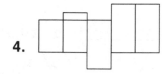

5.

6.

B **Use spelling words to complete the puzzle.**

Across

2. the ocean

4. what your eyes do

6. I ___ a horse at
   the ranch.

7. a bucket

Down

1. light in color

3. I ___ hot dogs for
   dinner last night.

5. comes after seven

6. a street

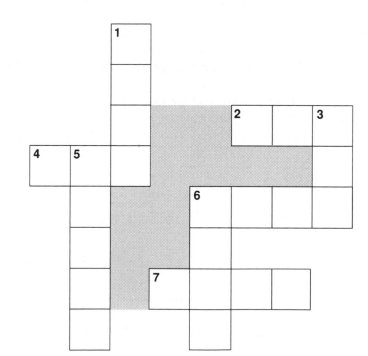

40

Lesson 10   Words with *ea*

DAY 1

breath	thread	feather	weather
spread	ready	heavy	leather

A **Fill in each blank with a spelling word.**

1. Let's _____ out the food on the picnic table.

2. This chair is very _____.

3. A _____ fell off the duck's back.

4. Can you _____ the needle without your glasses?

5. Are you _____ to go to the store?

6. I was out of _____ at the end of the race.

7. The _____ will be hot and sunny today.

8. Do you like this _____ belt?

B **Write a spelling word under each picture.**

1. _____   2. _____   3. _____

C **Circle the letters that are the same in all the spelling words.**

breath   spread   thread   ready   feather   heavy   weather   leather

D **Write the spelling words that name things you can touch.**

1. _____   2. _____   3. _____

Name _____

41

Lesson 10

Words with *ea*

breath	thread	feather	weather
spread	ready	heavy	leather

A Fill in the boxes with the correct spelling words.

1.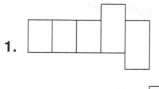

2.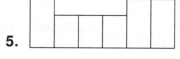

3.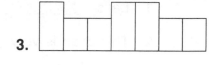

4.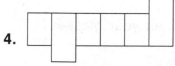

5.

6.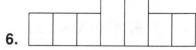

7.

8.

B Write each spelling word beside its clue.

_____ **1.** what most shoes are made of

_____ **2.** can be rainy, sunny, cloudy, stormy, or cold

_____ **3.** how you put butter on bread

_____ **4.** what you use with a needle to sew clothes

_____ **5.** the air you breathe in or out

_____ **6.** one of what a chicken has instead of fur

C Write the spelling words in alphabetical order.

1. _____ 2. _____ 3. _____

4. _____ 5. _____ 6. _____

7. _____ 8. _____

Lesson 10

DAY 3

Words with *ea*

breath	thread	feather	weather
spread	ready	heavy	leather

A Find each hidden word from the list.

breath	ready	weather	trail
spread	feather	leather	plain
thread	heavy	mail	brain

```
j a s o n i f e a t h e r s l m y s
s o n h r y a n s f r i t e e n d p
t h e e y p b r a i n l r a a y t r
o g e a t h e r i n t h a e t s w e
t i m v m i b r e a t h i g h p o a
h o l y t h e y l i k e l t e o l d
r i s t e n t o s t o r i e r s t h
e a p l a i n w e a t h e r t j a s
a o n s m o m t a m m y r e a d s t
d o t h e m a i l m s h r e a d y e
```

B Use the correct spelling words to complete the story.

I helped my uncle make a cement porch. It wasn't as hard as I thought it

would be. When the _____ was dry and sunny, we marked off

a place for the porch. Then we got the ground _____.

My uncle mixed the cement. Then we poured it in the place we

had marked. We had to work fast before the cement became hard. We

_____ it with a tool called a trowel. By the next day, the porch

was dry. My uncle and I were proud of the porch we made.

Name _____

DAY
4

Words with *ea*

breath	thread	feather	weather
spread	ready	heavy	leather

A Find the missing letters. Then write the word.

1. s p __ __ __ __   _____

2. b r __ __ __ h   _____

3. f __ __ t h __ __   _____

B Use each spelling word in a sentence.

breath _____

spread _____

thread _____

ready _____

feather _____

heavy _____

weather _____

leather _____

C One word is wrong in each sentence. Circle the wrong word. Then fill in the blank with a spelling word that makes sense.

1. The sofa is very green to pick up.   _____

2. I sew with a needle and rope.   _____

3. She threw the jelly on the toast.   _____

4. We found a duck's tail near the pond.   _____

5. My belt is made of sand.   _____

foot	stood	food	booth	thief
hook	hood	noon	tooth	chief
wood	crook	bloom	goose	niece
brook	cook	loose	proof	piece

A Write a spelling word under each picture.

1. _____ 2. _____ 3. _____

B Fill in each blank with a spelling word.

1. My rat got out of its cage, and now it's _____!

2. Let's eat lunch at 12 _____.

3. I will not pull a _____ out of a fish's mouth.

4. A person that steals is a _____.

5. I need _____ that you are old enough to drive.

6. May I have a _____ of your birthday cake?

7. We need more _____ for our fire.

8. My _____ and nephew are coming to visit me.

9. That jacket also has a _____.

10. I'm helping my mom make the _____ for dinner tonight.

11. We are setting up a _____ at our county fair.

12. The flowers will _____ in spring.

Name _____

field	road	ate	breath	feather
shield	rode	eight	spread	heavy
brief	pail	see	thread	weather
yield	pale	sea	ready	leather

C **Write the spelling words that rhyme with the word pair.**

1. load   mode   _____

2. tea   free   _____

3. late   rate   _____

4. mail   tail   _____

5. thief   chief   _____

D **Use the correct spelling words to complete the story.**

I was working outside in a large _____ with several of my friends. We were picking strawberries. Suddenly the _____ started to change. Clouds were forming and a _____ rain began to fall. I _____ my coat across as many of my friends as I could, and we got _____ to run. The coat was our only _____ against the rain and hail. We picked up our buckets that were filled to the top with strawberries. The buckets were so full that it was difficult to carry them.

We ran across the road and jumped in our car. It was hard for us to catch our _____ because we were so tired and wet. It was hard to see through the rain, so we drove home slowly. We remember that day every time we eat strawberries.

DAY 1

Words with *ear*

heard	earn	earth	yearn
learn	pearl	search	early

A Fill in each blank with a spelling word.

1. You have to wake up _____ to go to school on time.

2. The diver found a _____ in the oyster.

3. Dirt is also called _____.

4. I _____ to win first place.

5. We had to _____ for our lost kitten.

6. How much money do you _____ on your paper route?

7. I _____ that story when I was a child.

8. What did you _____ in school today?

B Circle the letters that are the same in all the spelling words.

heard   learn   earn   pearl   earth   search   yearn   early

C Write the spelling words that rhyme with the word pair.

1. bird   third   _____

2. curl   girl   _____

3. church   perch   _____

4. burn   fern   _____

5. stern   earn   _____

6. curly   surly   _____

7. birth   worth   _____

Name _____

Lesson 11

Words with *ear*

heard	earn	earth	yearn
learn	pearl	search	early

A **Put an *X* on the word that is <u>not</u> the same.**

1. heard	heard	hard	heard	heard
2. learn	lean	learn	learn	learn
3. earn	earn	earn	earm	earn
4. pearl	qearl	pearl	pearl	pearl
5. earth	earth	earht	earth	earth
6. search	sarch	search	search	search
7. yearn	yearn	yarn	yearn	yearn

B **Write a spelling word under each picture.**

1. _____   2. _____   3. _____

C **Write the spelling words that name things you <u>cannot</u> touch.**

1. _____   2. _____   3. _____

4. _____   5. _____   6. _____

D **Write the spelling words in alphabetical order.**

1. _____   2. _____   3. _____   4. _____

5. _____   6. _____   7. _____   8. _____

Lesson 11   Words with *ear*

heard	earn	earth	yearn
learn	pearl	search	early

A   **Use the correct spelling words to complete the story.**

Have you _____ how an oyster makes a _____?

An oyster is an animal that lives in the ocean. It starts with an accident

_____ in an oyster's life. A bit of sand gets in the oyster's shell. The

lining of the shell starts to cover the piece of sand. Layers of the shell lining

build up over the years. Finally, a pearl is formed.

You have to look in many oysters to find just one pearl. But the

_____ is worth it. A perfect, round pearl is worth a lot of money.

People have studied oysters to _____ how to get them to make

pearls. A piece of sand or shell can be put into young oysters. Then the

oysters are kept in special cages. After a few years, about one out of twenty

oysters will have a beautiful pearl inside its shell.

B   **Fill in the boxes with the correct spelling words.**

1.

2.

3.

4.

5.

6.

7.

8.

Name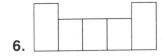

DAY 4

Words with *ear*

heard	earn	earth	yearn
learn	pearl	search	early

A Find the missing letters. Then write the word.

1. ___ e a r d   _____

2. ___ ___ ___ t h   _____

B Write each spelling word beside its clue.

_____ **1.** to get to know something by study or practice

_____ **2.** to deserve or win

_____ **3.** a white jewel formed in oysters

_____ **4.** to want something very much

_____ **5.** to look for something

_____ **6.** dirt or soil

C Use each spelling word in a sentence.

heard _____

learn _____

earn _____

pearl _____

earth _____

search _____

yearn _____

early _____

DAY 1

Words with -*y*

cry	dry	fly	spy
fry	shy	sky	pry

A **Fill in each blank with a spelling word.**

1. The _____ is very blue today.

2. I need to _____ my wet clothes.

3. Let's _____ the fish over the campfire.

4. I began to _____ when I heard the bad news.

5. The puppy was so _____ that it hid behind the sofa.

6. I'm trying to swat that _____ away from me!

7. She had to _____ the lid off the jar.

8. You should not _____ on your friends.

B **Answer the questions with spelling words.**

1. Which words end with *ry*?

   _____ _____ _____ _____

2. Which words begin with *s*?

   _____ _____ _____

3. Which words do these words come from?

   pries _____   spies _____

   dries _____   cries _____

   fries _____   flies _____

C **Circle the letter that is the same in all the spelling words.**

cry   fry   dry   shy   fly   sky   spy   pry

Name _____

Words with -*y*

cry	dry	fly	spy
fry	shy	sky	pry

A **Put an *X* on the word that is <u>not</u> the same.**

1. cry	cry	cny	cry	cry
2. fry	fny	fry	fry	fry
3. dry	dry	dry	dry	bry
4. shy	shy	sby	shy	shy
5. fly	flg	fly	fly	fly

B **Fill in the boxes with the correct spelling words.**

1.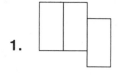

2.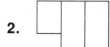

3.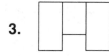

4.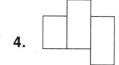

5.

6.

C **Use each spelling word in a sentence.**

cry _____

fry _____

dry _____

shy _____

fly _____

sky _____

spy _____

pry _____

Words with -*y*

cry	dry	fly	spy
fry	shy	sky	pry

A Use the correct spelling words to complete the story.

I love good _____ movies. They keep you on the edge of

your seat.

My favorite actor played a spy named James Bond. He had special

cars that could do everything but _____. Even his watch was full

of tricks.

In one movie, a man puts a deadly spider in James Bond's bed. You see the

spider crawl across Bond's chest. Whenever I see this part, I _____

out, "Don't move!" But things always turn out all right for him.

I'd love to meet this actor in person someday. But I'm sure I'd be too

_____ to even speak to him.

B Write the spelling words in alphabetical order.

1. _____   2. _____   3. _____   4. _____

5. _____   6. _____   7. _____   8. _____

C Complete each sentence. Use a dictionary if you need to.

1. "Cry" means _____.

2. "Spy" means _____.

3. "Shy" means _____.

4. "Pry" means _____.

Name _____

Words with -*y*

cry	dry	fly	spy
fry	shy	sky	pry

A Write the spelling word that matches its antonym (opposite).

1. ground   _____

2. outgoing   _____

3. laugh   _____

4. wet   _____

B Add *ing* to the spelling words below. Then write sentences using the new words.

cry   *crying*   *The baby is crying.*

dry   _____   _____

fly   _____   _____

spy   _____   _____

fry   _____   _____

pry   _____   _____

C Fill in each blank with a spelling word.

1. Write the word that belongs with cooking.

_____

2. Write the word that tells what birds do.

_____

3. Write the word that tells where clouds float.

_____

Homonyms

to	for	bear	flour
two	four	bare	flower

A **Fill in each blank with a spelling word.**

1. She walked outside in her _____ feet.

2. This cake calls for sifted _____.

3. Please open the door _____ me.

4. Half of a month is about _____ weeks.

5. Will you go with me _____ the party?

6. Two, _____ six, eight! Who do we appreciate?

7. Did you see that big _____ in the park?

8. His mother wore a pretty _____ on her blouse.

B **Fill in each blank with a spelling word.**

1. Write the words that have both *a* and *e* in them.

   _____   _____

2. Write the shortest word. _____

3. Write the longest word. _____

4. Write the words that are numbers.

   _____   _____

C **Write a spelling word under each picture.**

  4

1. _____ 2. _____ 3. _____

Name _____

Homonyms

to	for	bear	flour
two	four	bare	flower

A Fill in the boxes with the correct spelling words.

1.
2.
3.

4.
5.
6.

B Circle the correct answer to complete the sentence.

1. The four pairs of words in this lesson are _____.

   synonyms   homonyms   antonyms

2. The word _____ has as many letters as the number it is.

   for   four

3. One of the *b* words is an animal. It is _____.

   bear   bare

4. One of the words is visited by bees. It is _____.

   flour   flower

5. It is _____ that two of the words are living things.

   true   false

C Write the spelling words in alphabetical order.

1. _____   2. _____   3. _____   4. _____

5. _____   6. _____   7. _____   8. _____

DAY 3

to	for	bear	flour
two	four	bare	flower

A Find each hidden word from the list.

to	four	flour	coast
two	bear	flower	load
for	bare	toast	road

```
p  o  d  f  b  o  u  r  r  h  f  a  s  f  o  u  r
j  u  d  y  a  a  n  d  o  d  l  o  a  d  e  n  i
s  e  a  n  r  d  b  a  a  r  o  b  a  r  a  a  n
d  b  t  r  e  b  a  r  d  a  u  a  n  c  d  a  t
f  l  s  o  p  f  h  e  r  n  r  e  s  o  h  e  w
o  y  h  a  v  l  e  f  i  f  t  h  a  a  d  d  o
r  s  i  x  t  o  a  s  t  t  h  g  r  s  a  d  e
r  s  a  n  d  w  i  l  i  k  e  t  h  t  e  m  a
l  l  v  e  r  e  y  m  u  c  h  t  h  e  y  d  o
l  o  t  s  o  r  f  t  h  g  o  o  b  e  a  r  d
```

B Write each spelling word beside its clue.

_____   **1.** this is used to make bread

_____   **2.** an animal with thick fur, short legs, and sharp claws

_____   **3.** the number after three

_____   **4.** not covered

_____   **5.** the number after one

_____   **6.** the blossom of a plant

Name _____

Homonyms

to	for	bear	flour
two	four	bare	flower

A **Use the correct spelling words to complete the story.**

We were on a campout. It was my turn _____ go into town for

food. The store was just _____ miles from camp, so I went on foot.

On the way, I stopped to admire a _____. Right beside the

flowers were some paw prints. I bent down to study the prints. I'd seen them

before in a book.

They looked like _____ tracks. Bears! I ran _____ my

life back to camp.

B **Use each spelling word in a sentence.**

to _____

two _____

for _____

four _____

bear _____

bare _____

flour _____

flower _____

C **Find the missing letters. Then write the word.**

1. f ___ ___ ___ e r _____

2. b ___ ___ r _____

Words with *eigh*

sleigh	weigh	neighbor	eighty
freight	weight	neigh	freighter

A Fill in each blank with a spelling word.

1. A _____ is a ship that carries cargo.

2. Let's ride a _____ through the snow.

3. The doctor will _____ you on the scale.

4. The _____ on the truck was fruits and vegetables.

5. The hog's _____ was 300 pounds.

6. My _____ next door has a very nice yard.

7. The horse gave a loud _____ and threw back its head.

8. There were _____ people on the jet plane.

B Circle the letters that are the same in all the spelling words.

sleigh   freight   weigh   weight   neighbor   neigh   eighty   freighter

C Write the spelling words that rhyme with the word pair.

1. day   ray   _____

2. date   rate   _____

D One word is wrong in each sentence. Circle the wrong word. Then fill in the blank with a spelling word that makes sense.

1. She is my next-door tractor.   _____

2. How much does the box height?   _____

3. It's fun to ride a snake in the snow.   _____

Name _____

DAY 2

Words with *eigh*

sleigh	weigh	neighbor	eighty
freight	weight	neigh	freighter

A Find each hidden word from the list.

sleigh	weight	eighty	shade
freight	neighbor	freighter	flake
weigh	neigh	blade	snake

```
s  s  o  t  o  d  a  s  l  e  i  g  h  y  i  s  n
h  f  r  e  i  g  h  t  e  r  e  n  f  a  b  n  e
a  d  i  f  a  m  w  e  i  g  h  w  l  o  l  r  i
d  k  i  r  n  g  h  a  r  d  o  n  a  t  a  h  g
e  i  s  e  a  g  w  e  i  g  h  t  k  a  d  i  h
n  s  o  i  o  n  i  l  w  i  l  l  e  b  e  e  b
b  a  c  g  k  a  t  g  s  e  a  w  e  l  l  w  o
i  t  h  h  v  a  l  h  e  r  s  n  a  k  e  i  r
a  a  n  t  d  o  r  t  b  a  r  b  a  r  a  l  a
n  e  i  g  h  w  l  e  r  a  n  e  i  g  h  t  y
```

B Write a spelling word under each picture.

1. _____ 2. _____ 3. _____

C Write the spelling words in alphabetical order.

1. _____ 2. _____ 3. _____ 4. _____

5. _____ 6. _____ 7. _____ 8. _____

Words with *eigh*

sleigh	weigh	neighbor	eighty
freight	weight	neigh	freighter

A **Use the correct spelling words to complete the story.**

I had a _____ once who was almost _____ years

old. He liked to tell me stories. When he was a young man, he used to work

on a _____. A freighter is a ship that carries freight. His job was

to _____ the freight as it was loaded on the ship. Sometimes

the freight would weigh a lot. Then he would have to figure out how much to

charge the owners of the freight.

B **Write each spelling word beside its clue.**

_____ **1.** goods that are carried by land, sea, or air

_____ **2.** someone who lives close to you

_____ **3.** the amount that something weighs

_____ **4.** the sound a horse makes

_____ **5.** a ship carrying cargo

_____ **6.** what you do to find the weight of something

_____ **7.** something to ride in through the snow

_____ **8.** the number after 79

C **Write the spelling words that name things you can touch.**

1. _____   2. _____   3. _____

4. _____

Name _____

61

Words with *eigh*

sleigh	weigh	neighbor	eighty
freight	weight	neigh	freighter

A Put an *X* on the word that is **not** the same.

1.	sleigh	sleigh	sleihg	sleigh	sleigh
2.	freight	freight	freight	freighf	freight
3.	weigh	wiegh	weigh	weigh	weigh
4.	weight	weight	weight	weight	weighf
5.	neighbor	neighbor	neighdor	neighbor	neighbor
6.	neigh	neigh	neijh	neigh	neigh
7.	eighty	eihgty	eighty	eighty	eighty

B Circle the correct answer that matches its clue.

1. Seventy-nine comes before this.

    eight   eighty

2. Most trucks on the road carry this.

    sleigh   freight   neighbor

3. This is a person that lives close to you.

    freight   neighbor   sleigh

4. This is something that you ride in.

    neigh   sleigh   weigh

5. You find this out when you read a scale.

    weight   freight   eight

6. This is a ship that carries cargo.

    freight   sleigh   freighter

Words with *kn-*

kneel	knife	knot	knight
knock	knit	knob	knack

A **Fill in each blank with a spelling word.**

1. The door _____ fell off when I touched it.

2. Did you _____ that pretty sweater?

3. We learned how to tie a _____ with a rope.

4. She has a _____ for saying the right thing.

5. A _____ was a soldier in King Arthur's court.

6. The new _____ is very sharp.

7. Please _____ before you come in my room.

8. You have to _____ down to work in the garden.

B **Circle the letters that are the same in all the spelling words.**

kneel   knock   knife   knit   knot   knob   knight   knack

C **Write the spelling word that rhymes with the word pair.**

1. sock   rock   _____

2. fit   kit   _____

3. bite   kite   _____

4. cot   lot   _____

5. wife   life   _____

6. feel   peel   _____

7. cob   sob   _____

8. sack   pack   _____

Name _____

Words with *kn-*

kneel	knife	knot	knight
knock	knit	knob	knack

A Put an *X* on the word that is <u>not</u> the same.

1.	kneel	knell	kneel	kneel	kneel
2.	knock	knock	knock	knock	kneck
3.	knife	knife	knite	knife	knife
4.	knit	knit	knit	kmit	knit
5.	knot	knof	knot	knot	knot
6.	knob	knod	knob	knob	knob
7.	knight	knight	knighf	knight	knight
8.	knack	knack	knack	kacnk	knack

B Write each spelling word beside its clue.

_____   **1.** a kitchen tool used for cutting

_____   **2.** a round handle for opening a door

_____   **3.** a talent for doing something

_____   **4.** a soldier who fought for a king or queen

_____   **5.** a fastening or a tangle

_____   **6.** to hit or rap

_____   **7.** to rest on your knees

_____   **8.** to loop yarn together for clothes

C Write the spelling words that name things you can touch.

1. _____   2. _____   3. _____   4. _____

Words with *kn-*

DAY 3

kneel	knife	knot	knight
knock	knit	knob	knack

A **Use the correct spelling words to complete the story.**

Have you heard this fairy tale? In the woods lived a man who had a

_____ for solving problems. One day there was a _____

at the man's door. The king had come to ask the man to help his daughter, the

princess. Someone had put a spell on the princess and turned her into a cat.

The man went back to the castle with the king. He asked to see the cat.

Then he pulled a _____ out of his pocket. He cut off a bit of the

cat's hair. He spoke some words of magic. The cat turned back into the

princess.

The king was very happy. He had the man _____ before him

and made him a _____ of the royal court.

B **Write a spelling word under each picture.**

1. _____   2. _____   3. _____

C **Fill in the boxes with the correct spelling words.**

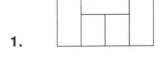 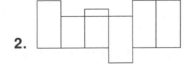 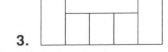

1.   2.   3.

4.   5.   6.

Name _____

Words with *kn-*

DAY 4

kneel	knife	knot	knight
knock	knit	knob	knack

A Find the missing letters. Then write the word.

1. k ___ ___ ___ ___ t   _____

2. k ___ ___ ___ e   _____

B Match each spelling word with a related word.

_____	**1.** kneel	**a.**	fork
_____	**2.** knock	**b.**	door
_____	**3.** knife	**c.**	talent
_____	**4.** knit	**d.**	rap
_____	**5.** knot	**e.**	soldier
_____	**6.** knob	**f.**	sweater
_____	**7.** knight	**g.**	rope
_____	**8.** knack	**h.**	bend

C Answer the questions with spelling words.

1. Which words end with *ck*?

   _____   _____

2. Which words have the long *i* sound?

   _____   _____

3. Which words have the short *o* sound?

   _____   _____   _____

4. Which word has the long *e* sound?   _____

heard	earth	cry	fly	to
learn	search	fry	sky	two
earn	yearn	dry	spy	for
pearl	early	shy	pry	four

A Write a spelling word under each picture.

1. _____ 2. _____ 3. _____

B Fill in each blank with a spelling word.

1. Open the oyster shell, and look at the shiny _____.

2. If you go with us, you'll have to wake up _____.

3. I love to _____ my kite with my friends.

4. The _____ is black, and I think it will storm.

5. You need to _____ your clothes before we leave.

6. What did you _____ in class today?

7. Please take care of the baby, or he will _____.

8. I only have _____ more hours before my date arrives.

9. We will _____ the eggs in the pan.

10. My sister's new puppy is very quiet and _____.

11. This package is _____ your brother.

12. Please give this letter _____ her.

Name _____

bear	sleigh	neighbor	kneel	knot
bare	freight	neigh	knock	knob
flour	weigh	eighty	knife	knight
flower	weight	freighter	knit	knack

C **Write the spelling words that rhyme with the word pair.**

1. block   clock   _____

2. rare   tear   _____

3. weigh   sleigh   _____

4. fit   sit   _____

5. feel   seal   _____

D **Use the correct spelling words to complete the story.**

Have you ever heard the story of King Arthur? The story says that he was a

King of England, and he had many soldiers. A soldier was called a _____.

Each knight had a _____ or a special way of taking care of the kingdom.

Some were good at sword fighting, and some even fought with a long stick called

a staff. When the knights put on their armor, the _____ of their

body would become much heavier. It's amazing that they could even move in

their armor!

Although the knights would fight, they were also gentle. They could see the

beauty of a fresh _____ or have fun with their children as they rode

through the snow in a _____.

Lesson 16

Words with *wr-*

DAY 1

wrench	wrist	wreck	wren
wring	wrong	wrestle	wreath

A Fill in each blank with a spelling word.

1. She said her messy room was a _____.

2. Do you like the _____ on our door?

3. The bird singing outside is a _____.

4. The puppies like to _____ around on the floor.

5. He began to _____ the water out of his clothes.

6. It is _____ to cheat on a test.

7. He broke his _____ in the football game.

8. I need a _____ to fix the sink.

B Write the spelling word that rhymes with the word pair.

1. sing   bring   _____

2. fist   list   _____

3. song   long   _____

4. deck   neck   _____

5. pen   ten   _____

6. teeth   sheath   _____

C Write a spelling word under each picture.

      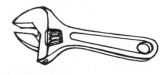

1. _____   2. _____   3. _____

Name _____

Words with *wr-*

wrench	wrist	wreck	wren
wring	wrong	wrestle	wreath

A Circle the letters that are the same in all the spelling words.

wrench   wring   wrist   wrong   wreck   wrestle   wren   wreath

B Which letter is silent in all the spelling words? _____

C Use spelling words to complete the puzzle.

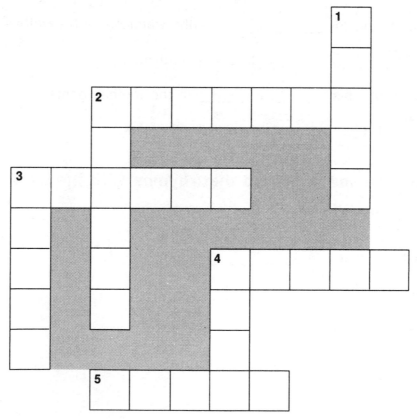

Across

2. to struggle with something

3. a tool

4. between the hand and arm

5. to squeeze out or twist

Down

1. Two cars had a ___.

2. a ring of leaves or branches

3. incorrect

4. a songbird

Words with *wr-*

wrench	wrist	wreck	wren
wring	wrong	wrestle	wreath

A **Use the correct spelling words to complete the story.**

My friend and I were riding in my car when we saw a line of cars ahead.
We knew something was _____. All of the cars in our lane began to
slow down. Then we saw a man standing on the side of the road. His car
had broken down. We were so glad it wasn't a bad _____. We
decided to stop and help him fix his car. I looked in my toolbox and found a
_____ and some other tools. After about twenty minutes, he was able
to start his car. He sure was happy that we stopped to help.

B **Match each spelling word with a related word.**

_____	1. wreath	a.	crash
_____	2. wren	b.	watch
_____	3. wrestle	c.	incorrect
_____	4. wreck	d.	bird
_____	5. wrong	e.	decoration
_____	6. wrist	f.	struggle
_____	7. wring	g.	tool
_____	8. wrench	h.	twist

C **Write the spelling words that name things you can touch.**

1. _____   2. _____

3. _____   4. _____

Name _____

Lesson 16   Words with *wr-*

wrench	wrist	wreck	wren
wring	wrong	wrestle	wreath

A Fill in the boxes with the correct spelling words.

1.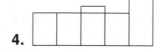

2.

3.

4.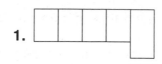

5.

6.

B Write the spelling words in alphabetical order.

1. _____ 2. _____ 3. _____ 4. _____

5. _____ 6. _____ 7. _____ 8. _____

C Use each spelling word in a sentence.

wrench _____

wring _____

wrist _____

wrong _____

wreck _____

wrestle _____

wren _____

wreath _____

D Find the missing letters. Then write the word.

1. ____ r ____ ____   _____

2. w r ____ ____ t   _____

72

Contractions with -*n't*

won't	isn't	didn't	hasn't
aren't	doesn't	wasn't	weren't

A **Fill in each blank with a spelling word.**

1. We _____ ready to leave yet.

2. One twin likes to paint, but the other twin _____.

3. I _____ feeling well last week.

4. He _____ be able to go with us.

5. She _____ eaten dinner yet.

6. _____ you the captain of the team last year?

7. Earth _____ the largest planet.

8. We almost won today, _____ we?

B **Circle the letters that are the same in all the spelling words.**

won't   aren't   isn't   doesn't   didn't   wasn't   hasn't   weren't

C **Answer each question.**

1. What word does *n't* stand for? _____

2. What are the words in this lesson called?

    homonyms.   contractions   compounds.

D **Find the missing letters. Then write the word.**

1. ___ r e ___ ' ___   _____

2. h ___ s n ' ___   _____

3. d ___ ___ ___ n ' t   _____

Name _____

73

Contractions with -*n't*

won't	isn't	didn't	hasn't
aren't	doesn't	wasn't	weren't

A The spelling words in this lesson are called contractions.
Match each contraction with its pair of words.

_____ **1.** isn't   **a.** were not

_____ **2.** doesn't   **b.** are not

_____ **3.** hasn't   **c.** will not

_____ **4.** weren't   **d.** did not

_____ **5.** won't   **e.** is not

_____ **6.** aren't   **f.** does not

_____ **7.** didn't   **g.** has not

B Put an *X* on the word that is <u>not</u> the same.

1. aren't	aren't	aren't	aren't	aern't
2. didn't	didn't	dibn't	didn't	didn't
3. won't	wou't	won't	won't	won't

C Use spelling words to complete the puzzle.

Across

3. is not

4. were not

5. has not

Down

1. did not

2. are not

DAY 3

Contractions with *-n't*

| won't | isn't | didn't | hasn't |
| aren't | doesn't | wasn't | weren't |

A Find each hidden word from the list. The contractions are written without an (').

won't	doesn't	hasn't	state
aren't	didn't	weren't	tame
isn't	wasn't	plate	flame

h	s	y	h	e	r	w	a	s	n	t	d	d	n	l	b	h
o	f	a	o	d	o	n	t	t	d	a	h	i	g	i	u	a
m	l	t	o	o	p	i	e	l	i	w	e	d	a	p	t	s
a	a	a	r	e	n	t	r	e	s	h	l	n	n	l	m	n
s	m	o	l	s	e	r	m	f	n	o	p	t	d	a	o	t
w	e	u	s	n	p	e	y	r	t	n	i	a	s	t	s	a
o	v	r	o	t	p	m	w	e	r	e	n	t	p	e	t	l
r	e	s	d	s	e	e	l	i	l	e	n	d	e	n	o	l
s	t	a	t	e	r	m	i	e	w	o	n	t	a	m	e	i

B Write the spelling words in alphabetical order.

1. _____ 2. _____ 3. _____ 4. _____

5. _____ 6. _____ 7. _____ 8. _____

C Circle the word that is the same as the top one.

won't	aren't	isn't	doesn't	didn't	wasn't	hasn't	weren't
bon't	aren't	isn'f	boesn't	dibn't	wasn't	basn't	waren't
won't	arem't	sin't	dosen't	didn't	wasm't	hasm't	weren't
dom't	anen't	isn't	daesn't	didn'f	wasn'f	hasn't	werem't
don'f	aren'f	ism't	doesn't	didm't	wosn't	hosn't	weren'f

Name _____

Contractions with -n't

won't	isn't	didn't	hasn't
aren't	doesn't	wasn't	weren't

A Fill in each blank with the correct spelling word.

1. She _____ have to leave early.
   isn't   doesn't

2. They _____ going to the zoo today.
   weren't   wasn't

3. He _____ the one who has the ball.
   aren't   isn't

4. It _____ been long since they left.
   weren't   hasn't

5. She _____ know how to use the new computer.
   didn't   hasn't

6. It _____ their fault that they were late.
   wasn't   weren't

7. They _____ be attending the party.
   doesn't   won't

8. _____ you excited about the trip?
   Isn't   Aren't

B Use the correct spelling words to complete the story.

My little brother is six years old. He likes to play baseball. He

_____ a very good player yet, but that _____ bother him.

He knows he'll get better with practice.

He is good at throwing the ball. But he _____ run to catch the

ball if it's far away. He also needs to practice batting. He struck out three

times in the last game he played.

I'm going to help him become a better player.

Homonyms

blew	hear	sale	knew
blue	here	sail	new

A Fill in each blank with a spelling word.

1. The store is having a _____ on clothes.

2. The truck _____ a tire and ran off the road.

3. He is _____ today to talk to you.

4. I _____ her when she was just a little girl.

5. Did you _____ what he said?

6. The sky is so clear and _____ today.

7. They will _____ around the world on a ship.

8. Are you a _____ student, or were you here last year?

B Circle the correct answer to complete the sentence.

1. The word pairs in this lesson are _____.

    synonyms   homonyms   antonyms

2. "Blue" and "blew" are not spelled alike, but they _____ .

    sound alike   feel alike   mean the same thing

3. The word that begins with a silent letter is _____ .

    sail   blew   here   knew

C Write the spelling words that rhyme with the word pair.

1. do   flew   _____

2. ear   dear   _____

3. pail   fail   _____

Name _____

Homonyms

blew	hear	sale	knew
blue	here	sail	new

A Fill in the boxes with the correct spelling words.

1.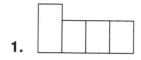

2.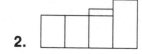

3.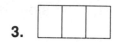

4.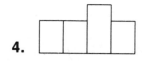

5.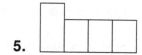

6.

7.

8.

B Write each spelling word beside its clue.

_____ **1.** the act of selling

_____ **2.** a "sheet" for catching wind on a ship

_____ **3.** not old

_____ **4.** where you are right now

_____ **5.** a color

_____ **6.** what the wind did yesterday

_____ **7.** what you do with your ears

_____ **8.** used to know

C Write the spelling words in alphabetical order.

1. _____ 2. _____ 3. _____ 4. _____

5. _____ 6. _____ 7. _____ 8. _____

Homonyms

blew	hear	sale	knew
blue	here	sail	new

A Use the correct spelling words to complete the story.

When I was ten years old, my family moved _____ to be near the ocean. This was a _____ kind of life for us at first, but we quickly became used to it. Now I love the water and sun and sand. I can wear shorts here all the time.

The family next door became our best friends. My mother says she _____ right away we'd get along. She was right! We enjoy the same things. We like to spend time on the beach. In the summer we _____ our boats together in the bay. On weekends we fish from the pier and cook our catch outdoors.

We're lucky to live by the ocean. We can go to the beach every day.

B Put an *X* on the word that is <u>not</u> the same.

1.	hear	hare	hear	hear	hoar
2.	sale	sale	sale	sael	sale
3.	knew	knew	knew	knew	know
4.	new	now	new	new	new
5.	blew	blew	blew	blow	blew
6.	blue	blue	bule	blue	blue
7.	here	here	here	heer	here
8.	sail	sali	sail	sail	sail

Name _____

DAY 4

Homonyms

blew	hear	sale	knew
blue	here	sail	new

A Find the missing letters. Then write the word.

1. b _____ _____ e   _____

2. _____ _____ l _____   _____

B Answer the questions with spelling words.

1. Which words end with *ew*?

_____   _____   _____

2. Which word does not have the letter *e* in it? _____

C Use each spelling word in a sentence.

blew _____

blue _____

hear _____

here _____

sale _____

sail _____

knew _____

new _____

D Write the spelling words that name things you <u>cannot</u> touch.

1. _____   2. _____   3. _____

4. _____   5. _____   6. _____

Contractions with -'ll and -'ve

I'll	she'll	I've	we've
you'll	he'll	you've	they've

A Fill in each blank with a spelling word.

1. My sister says _____ attend summer school.

2. If you tell me a secret, _____ never repeat it.

3. _____ got a quarter in my pocket.

4. You must be careful, or _____ hurt yourself.

5. _____ won all their games this year.

6. If _____ never been to the sea, you should go.

7. If a peacock wants to show off, _____ spread his tail feathers.

8. _____ got five people in our family.

B Circle the letters that are the same in all the spelling words.

I've   you've   we've   they've

C Answer each question.

1. What word does *'ve* stand for? _____

2. What word does *'ll* stand for? _____

D Find the missing letters. Then write the word.

1. ___ ___ e ' l l   _____

2. ___ ___ ___ ___ ' v e   _____

3. y ___ ___ ' ___ l   _____

Name _____

Lesson 19

Contractions with -'ll and -'ve

I'll	she'll	I've	we've
you'll	he'll	you've	they've

A Match each contraction with its pair of words.

_____ **1.** she'll   **a.** they have

_____ **2.** he'll   **b.** you will

_____ **3.** you'll   **c.** we have

_____ **4.** I'll   **d.** I have

_____ **5.** we've   **e.** she will

_____ **6.** they've   **f.** he will

_____ **7.** I've   **g.** I will

B Fill in the boxes with the correct spelling words.

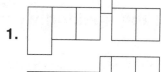

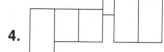

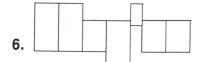

C Use spelling words to complete the puzzle.

Across	**Down**
1. they have	**2.** you have
4. I have	**3.** we have
5. she will	**4.** I will

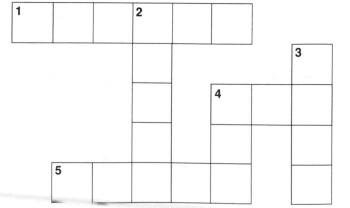

82

DAY 3

Contractions with -'ll and -'ve

I'll	she'll	I've	we've
you'll	he'll	you've	they've

A Find each hidden word from the list. The contractions are written without an (').

life	they've	she'll	wife	we've
you've	strike	you'll	bike	

```
s  o  m  e  w  h  e  r  e  o  v  e  r  t  h  y  e
r  w  e  l  l  a  l  i  f  e  i  n  b  o  w  o  w
a  y  u  p  h  i  g  h  t  h  e  r  e  s  a  u  l
a  s  n  d  y  t  h  a  t  i  h  l  e  t  a  v  w
r  h  d  o  o  f  w  i  f  e  o  l  n  h  c  e  e
i  e  n  a  u  l  u  k  a  b  l  y  e  s  o  v
m  l  e  l  l  w  h  e  r  e  o  v  e  y  r  t  e
h  l  e  v  l  r  b  i  k  e  a  i  n  v  b  o  w
s  k  i  e  s  a  r  e  b  l  u  e  a  e  n  d  t
h  e  d  r  e  a  s  t  r  i  k  e  m  s  t  h  a
```

B Use the correct spelling words to complete the story.

Some of us were talking about where _____ taken trips. I told the group that _____ never been out of the state. Others said _____ only seen one other state besides their own.

"That's hard to believe," said my friend. "You mean _____ never been out West or seen the Rocky Mountains?"

"No," I told him. "There's so much to see in my own state. I haven't had time to see anything else."

Name _____

DAY 4

Contractions with -'ll and -'ve

I'll	she'll	I've	we've
you'll	he'll	you've	they've

A **Fill in each blank with the correct spelling word.**

1. _____ be at school on time, won't you?
   You've   You'll

2. _____ never been there before.
   I'll   I've

3. _____ see you in town on Friday.
   She'll   We've

4. I know _____ be glad to see you.
   you've   he'll

5. _____ look both ways before I cross the street again.
   You've   I'll

6. _____ been very kind to each other.
   They've   You'll

7. _____ always tried to do our best work.
   We've   You'll

8. _____ been a joy to teach this year.
   He'll   You've

B **Complete each sentence.**

1. I've never thought _____.

2. We've always wished _____.

C **Write the spelling words in alphabetical order.**

1. _____   2. _____   3. _____   4. _____

5. _____   6. _____   7. _____   8. _____

Words with *-shes*

bushes	crushes	brushes	washes
wishes	flashes	dishes	fishes

A Fill in each blank with a spelling word.

1. That camera _____ in my face.

2. She _____ her hair before she goes to bed.

3. The cat _____ its paws until they are clean.

4. We planted three _____ in our yard.

5. The sign said, "You may have three _____."

6. The blender _____ ice very well.

7. Is it your turn to wash the _____?

8. My uncle _____ in the pond on his farm.

B Circle the letters that are the same in all the spelling words.

bushes   wishes   crushes   flashes   brushes   dishes   washes   fishes

C Write a spelling word under each picture.

1. _____   2. _____   3. _____

D Write the spelling words in alphabetical order.

1. _____   2. _____   3. _____   4. _____

5. _____   6. _____   7. _____   8. _____

Name _____

Words with -*shes*

bushes	crushes	brushes	washes
wishes	flashes	dishes	fishes

A Put an *X* on the word that is <u>not</u> the same.

1.	bushes	dushes	bushes	bushes	bushes
2.	wishes	wishes	wishes	mishes	wishes
3.	crushes	crushes	cnushes	crushes	crushes
4.	flashes	flashes	flashes	flashes	flaches
5.	brushes	brushes	drushes	brushes	brushes
6.	dishes	dishes	bishes	dishes	dishes
7.	washes	mashes	washes	washes	washes
8.	fishes	tishes	fishes	fishes	fishes

B Write each spelling word beside its clue.

_____ 1. what a blender does to ice

_____ 2. plates, bowls, and cups

_____ 3. what the bulb on a camera does

_____ 4. hopeful dreams

_____ 5. more than one brush

_____ 6. what a washer does

_____ 7. what one does with a rod and reel

_____ 8. shrubs or large woody plants

C Write the spelling words that name things you can touch.

1. _____ 2. _____ 0. _____

DAY 3

Words with -*shes*

bushes	crushes	brushes	washes
wishes	flashes	dishes	fishes

A **Use the correct spelling words to complete the story.**

I know a man who loves to cook, so he opened a small cafe. The cafe is a few miles out of town. He serves very good food there. But it keeps him busy all the time.

On his day off, he _____ for trout to serve at the cafe. He cleans the fish himself. His wife makes the breads and desserts. She also helps seat the guests. Their son helps wash the _____. The oldest daughter _____ and irons the napkins and tablecloths. Sometimes she helps serve the food. Much of what they cook is grown in their own garden.

The man says he _____ he had more free time. "But if I did," he says, "I'd probably just spend it cooking."

B **Write the simplest form of each spelling word.**

1. _____ 2. _____ 3. _____ 4. _____

5. _____ 6. _____ 7. _____ 8. _____

C **Fill in the boxes with the correct spelling words.**

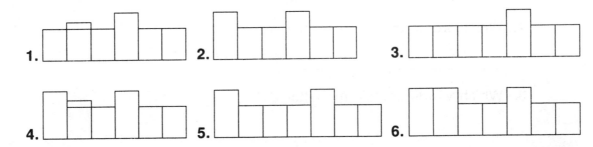

1.

2.

3.

4.

5.

6.

Name _____

Words with -*shes*

bushes	crushes	brushes	washes
wishes	flashes	dishes	fishes

A Find the missing letters. Then write the word.

1. b r __ __ __ __ __   _____

2. __ l __ __ __ __ __   _____

3. w i __ __ __ __   _____

B Use each spelling word in a sentence.

bushes _____

wishes _____

crushes _____

flashes _____

brushes _____

dishes _____

washes _____

fishes _____

C Answer the questions with spelling words.

1. Which words begin with two consonants?

   _____   _____   _____

2. Which words contain the letter *a*?

   _____   _____

3. Which words contain the letter *i*?

   _____   _____   _____

wrench	wreck	won't	didn't	blew
wring	wrestle	aren't	wasn't	blue
wrist	wren	isn't	hasn't	hear
wrong	wreath	doesn't	weren't	here

A Write a spelling word under each picture.

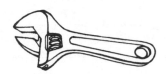  

1. _____ 2. _____ 3. _____

B Fill in each blank with a spelling word.

1. _____ that your mother over there?

2. I called her, but she _____ there.

3. Are your eyes _____ or brown?

4. The cars went too fast and caused a _____.

5. The kittens like to play and _____ with each other.

6. I think I put the _____ answer on the test.

7. _____ out your swimsuit before you hang it up to dry.

8. I put a _____ on my front door.

9. Did you _____ that loud noise outside?

10. The small flags _____ in the wind.

11. They will be _____ at two o'clock today.

12. He _____ called me back yet.

Name _____

sale	I'll	I've	bushes	brushes
sail	you'll	you've	wishes	dishes
knew	she'll	we've	crushes	washes
new	he'll	they've	flashes	fishes

C Write the spelling words that rhyme with the word pair.

1. rail   tail   _____

2. few   true   _____

3. wishes   fishes   _____

4. clashes   splashes   _____

5. dishes   wishes   _____

D Use the correct spelling words to complete the story.

Our club needed money for new band uniforms. We decided to have a

bake sale. We made about $200 from the sale. Our club leader told us,

"_____ done a good job so far, but the club still needs more money

for the uniforms. _____ need to make about $500 more." Whew!

It seemed like a lot of money, but we put our heads together to think of other

ways that we could make money. One person from the club said we should

trim _____ and trees to earn more money. We agreed that this

was a good idea. After we finished trimming, we counted our money. Our

_____ had come true! "_____ made enough money to

buy the uniforms!" we said to each other. The leader of our club was very

proud of us.

Words with -xes

boxes	fixes	taxes	mixes
foxes	waxes	axes	sixes

A **Fill in each blank with a spelling word.**

1. My dad _____ the floor to make it shine.

2. We pay _____ each year to help support our government.

3. There are many cake _____ to choose from.

4. Please count by twos and _____.

5. We piled the _____ on top of each other.

6. A plumber _____ stopped-up sinks.

7. Lumberjacks use _____ to cut down trees.

8. The farmer put up a fence to keep the _____ out.

B **Circle the letters that are the same in all the spelling words.**

boxes   foxes   fixes   waxes   taxes   axes   mixes   sixes

C **Write the spelling words in alphabetical order.**

1. _____ 2. _____ 3. _____ 4. _____

5. _____ 6. _____ 7. _____ 8. _____

D **Write the spelling words that name things you can touch.**

1. _____ 2. _____ 3. _____

4. _____ 5. _____

Name _____

Lesson 21   Words with *-xes*

boxes	fixes	taxes	mixes
foxes	waxes	axes	sixes

A   **Write the simplest form of each spelling word.**

1. _____ 2. _____ 3. _____ 4. _____

5. _____ 6. _____ 7. _____ 8. _____

B   **Use the correct spelling words to complete the story.**

I like to go to the dock to watch the ships unload. They bring goods from all parts of the world.

The goods come in _____. They're unpacked and sold here. But before the boxes can be unloaded, _____ must be paid on them.

The boxes all have numbers so that no one _____ them up. I like to imagine what's in the boxes.

C   **Write a spelling word under each picture.**

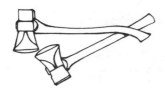  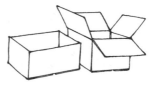

1. _____ 2. _____ 3. _____ 4. _____

D   **Find the missing letters. Then write the word.**

1. f o ___ ___ ___   _____

2. a ___ ___ ___   _____

Lesson 21

Words with -*xes*

boxes	fixes	taxes	mixes
foxes	waxes	axes	sixes

A Find each hidden word from the list.

boxes	waxes	mixes	spine
foxes	taxes	sixes	ripe
fixes	axes	vine	stripe

```
j  a  c  k  a  s  p  i  n  e  n  d  j  r  i  p  e
m  i  l  l  w  e  n  t  u  p  t  h  w  e  h  i  l
i  l  t  o  f  e  t  c  h  a  p  a  a  i  l  o  f
x  w  a  t  e  b  o  x  e  s  r  j  x  a  c  k  o
e  f  t  a  x  e  s  e  l  l  d  o  e  w  n  a  x
s  n  d  b  r  o  k  e  h  i  s  c  s  r  o  w  e
n  a  n  d  j  f  i  x  e  s  i  l  l  c  a  m  s
e  t  u  m  b  l  i  n  g  a  x  e  s  a  f  t  e
r  t  h  e  n  j  s  t  r  i  p  e  a  c  k  g  o
s  i  x  e  s  t  u  p  a  n  d  h  o  v  i  n  e
```

B Write each spelling word beside its clue.

_____   **1.** repairs or makes something right

_____   **2.** tools for chopping wood

_____   **3.** polishes for cars and furniture

_____   **4.** cardboard containers

_____   **5.** numbers

_____   **6.** furry-tailed animals

_____   **7.** blends together

_____   **8.** money we pay the government

Name _____

93

Lesson 21

DAY 4

Words with -*xes*

boxes	fixes	taxes	mixes
foxes	waxes	axes	sixes

A Put an *X* on the word that is <u>not</u> the same.

1.	boxes	doxes	boxes	boxes	boxes
2.	foxes	foxes	foxes	toxes	foxes
3.	fixes	fixes	fizes	fixes	fixes
4.	waxes	maxes	waxes	waxes	waxes
5.	taxes	taxes	taxes	faxes	taxes
6.	axes	axes	axes	axes	oxes
7.	mixes	mixes	mixes	wixes	mixes

B Write the spelling words that can either be nouns or verbs.

1. _____   2. _____   3. _____

4. _____   5. _____

C Use spelling words to complete the puzzle.

Across

1. He ___ the floor each week.

4. containers

5. the numbers after the fives

Down

2. chopping tools

3. animals with furry tails

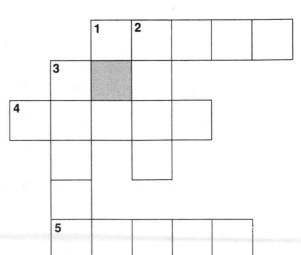

94

DAY 1

Words with *-ches*

branches	stitches	churches	crutches
speeches	scratches	catches	matches

A Fill in each blank with a spelling word.

1. The dog _____ its fur.

2. The outfielder _____ the ball.

3. We will need some _____ to light the fire.

4. The president makes many _____ each year.

5. The cut on my hand needed _____.

6. The strong winds broke the tree's _____.

7. He had to use _____ until his broken leg had mended.

8. I like to visit old _____.

B Circle the letters that are the same in all the spelling words.

branches	speeches	stitches	scratches
churches	catches	crutches	matches

C Write a spelling word under each picture.

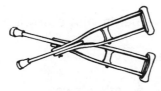      

1. _____   2. _____   3. _____

D Find the missing letters. Then write the word.

1. c ___ u t ___ ___ e s   _____

2. s t ___ ___ ___ ___ e s   _____

Name _____

Lesson 22

Words with -*ches*

branches	stitches	churches	crutches
speeches	scratches	catches	matches

A Find each hidden word from the list.

branches	scratches	crutches	bite
speeches	churches	matches	drive
stitches	catches	wise	why

```
c a t c h e s o s l d k i n g c o s
l e w a s a m e c r u t c h e s r p
r y o l e s o u r l a n d a m e r e
m a t c h e s r a y d r i v e w o e
l e s o u l w a t s h e h e c i a c
l l e d f o r h c h u r c h e s i h
s t i t c h e s h s p i b i t e p e
h e c a l l e d e f o r h i s b o s
w l a n d h e c s a l w h y l e d f
o r b r a n c h e s h i s f i d d l
```

B Write each spelling word beside its clue.

_____ **1.** the parts of a tree that have leaves

_____ **2.** in-and-out movements with a sewing needle

_____ **3.** what a baseball player does

_____ **4.** marks made by a cat's claws

_____ **5.** talks given to an audience

_____ **6.** used for support if a leg is broken

_____ **7.** used for starting fires

96

Words with *-ches*

branches	stitches	churches	crutches
speeches	scratches	catches	matches

A   **Put an *X* on the word that is <u>not</u> the same.**

1. branches	branches	brenches	branches	branches
2. speeches	speeches	speeches	squeeches	speeches
3. stitches	stitshes	stitches	stitches	stitches
4. scratches	scratches	scretches	scratches	scratches
5. churches	churches	churches	churches	charches
6. catches	catches	catches	cotches	catches
7. crutches	cnutches	crutches	crutches	crutches
8. matches	matches	watches	matches	matches

B   **Write the spelling words in alphabetical order.**

1. _____   2. _____   3. _____   4. _____

5. _____   6. _____   7. _____   8. _____

C   **Use the correct spelling words to complete the story.**

Every summer my family has a big picnic in the park. I always enjoy visiting

with my cousin, but I will never forget the time we decided to explore the park.

We hiked on the trails and climbed the _____ of a large tree. The

limbs of the trees left red _____ on our legs. Then when my cousin

climbed down from the tree, she slipped. She cut her leg, but she did not need

_____. That was the last time we went exploring!

Name _____

Words with *-ches*

branches	stitches	churches	crutches
speeches	scratches	catches	matches

A Write the simplest form of each spelling word.

1. _____ 2. _____ 3. _____ 4. _____

5. _____ 6. _____ 7. _____ 8. _____

B Match each spelling word with a related word.

_____ 1. branches   a. doctor

_____ 2. speeches   b. ball

_____ 3. stitches   c. tree

_____ 4. scratches   d. president

_____ 5. churches   e. broken leg

_____ 6. catches   f. weddings

_____ 7. crutches   g. cat

C Use each spelling word in a sentence.

branches _____

speeches _____

stitches _____

scratches _____

churches _____

catches _____

crutches _____

matches _____

Words with -ies

pennies	cherries	ponies	cities
babies	berries	puppies	guppies

A **Fill in each blank with a spelling word.**

1. I have been to several large _____.

2. Some _____ grow on vines.

3. The _____ on the tree look ripe to me.

4. Small horses are called _____.

5. _____ are good fish for an aquarium.

6. The dog had five _____.

7. A nursery is where you'll find _____.

8. I'll trade you a dime for ten _____.

B **Circle the letters that are the same in all the spelling words.**

pennies babies cherries berries ponies puppies cities guppies

C **Change the plural *ies* in the spelling words to the singular ending *y*. Write the singular words in the blanks.**

Plural   **Singular**

1. pennies   _____

2. babies   _____

3. cherries   _____

4. berries   _____

5. ponies   _____

6. puppies   _____

7. cities   _____

Name _____

Lesson 23

DAY 2

Words with *-ies*

pennies	cherries	ponies	cities
babies	berries	puppies	guppies

A **Use the correct spelling words to complete the story.**

One spring I went to visit my friend. She lives in a small town. I was so excited to visit her because I have always lived in large _____. She said that we were going to a carnival. "What's a carnival?" I thought to myself. I soon found out.

There were games, rides, food, and even animals at the carnival. One of the games I played only cost me ten _____. My friend and I rode _____ and ate ice cream sundaes with _____ on top.

B **Write the spelling words that name things you can touch.**

1. _____ 2. _____ 3. _____ 4. _____

5. _____ 6. _____ 7. _____ 8. _____

C **Match each spelling word with a related word.**

_____ 1. pennies   **a.** horses

_____ 2. babies   **b.** coins

_____ 3. cherries   **c.** traffic

_____ 4. berries   **d.** crib

_____ 5. ponies   **e.** water

_____ 6. puppies   **f.** vines

_____ 7. cities   **g.** pits

_____ 8. guppies   **h.** dogs

100

Lesson 23

DAY 3

Words with *-ies*

pennies	cherries	ponies	cities
babies	berries	puppies	guppies

A Use spelling words to complete the puzzle.

Across

3. small fish

6. big towns

7. very young children

Down

1. baby dogs

2. red fruits with pits

4. cents

5. small horses

B Write a spelling word under each picture.

1. _____   2. _____   3. _____

Name _____

101

Words with *-ies*

pennies	cherries	ponies	cities
babies	berries	puppies	guppies

A Fill in the boxes with the correct spelling words.

1.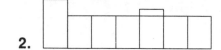

2.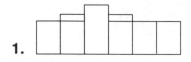

3.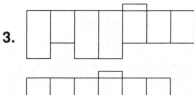

4.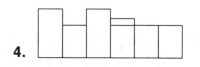

5.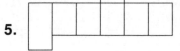

6.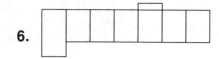

B Fill in each blank with a spelling word.

1. Write three words that can be pets.

   _____   _____   _____

2. Write two words that are fruits.

   _____   _____

3. Write the only word that contains the letter *a*. _____

4. Write the word that describes a place where people live. _____

5. Write the word for a type of money. _____

6. Write the word that begins with two consonants. _____

7. Write the only word that contains the letter *o*. _____

8. Write the words that have three different vowels.

   _____   _____

   _____   _____

Homonyms

hare	tail	sew	heal
hair	tale	sow	heel

A Fill in each blank with a spelling word.

1. I had to have a new _____ put on my shoe.

2. A _____ is a larger kind of rabbit.

3. Did you ever play "Pin the _____ on the donkey"?

4. My uncle told me a _____ about his younger days.

5. We will _____ the corn seed in the field today.

6. Can you _____ a button on your shirt?

7. The scratch won't take too long to _____.

8. I love to feel the wind through my _____.

B Circle the correct answer to complete the sentence.

1. "Sew" and "sow" are not spelled the same, but they _____.

    sound alike   mean the same   smell the same

2. The word pairs in this lesson are _____.

    homonyms   antonyms   synonyms

3. To "heal" is to _____.

    cure   fight   follow

C Find the missing letters. Then write the word.

1. t ___ i ___   _____

2. ___ o ___   _____

Name _____

Lesson 24   Homonyms

DAY 2

hare	tail	sew	heal
hair	tale	sow	heel

A Write the spelling words that rhyme with the word pair.

1. sail   rail   _____

2. know   grow   _____

3. feel   meal   _____

4. care   dare   _____

5. crow   low   _____

B Put an *X* on the word that is <u>not</u> the same.

1. hare	hane	hare	hare	hare
2. hair	hair	hair	hair	hain
3. tail	tail	fail	tail	tail
4. tale	tale	tele	tale	tale
5. sew	sew	sew	sow	sew
6. sow	sow	sow	osw	sow
7. heal	heal	heal	heal	hael
8. heel	heel	heel	beel	heel

C Write a spelling word under each picture.

1. _____   **2.** _____   **3.** _____

Lesson 24   Homonyms

hare	tail	sew	heal
hair	tale	sow	heel

A Write each spelling word beside its clue.

_____   **1.** to plant seeds

_____   **2.** an animal with long ears, a divided upper lip, and long hind legs for leaping

_____   **3.** to make healthy again

_____   **4.** the back part of the foot

_____   **5.** to join by stitches

_____   **6.** a story

_____   **7.** the bottom or end part of something

_____   **8.** fiber or fur

B Write the spelling words that name things you can touch.

1. _____   2. _____   3. _____   4. _____

C Write the spelling words in alphabetical order.

1. _____   2. _____   3. _____   4. _____

5. _____   6. _____   7. _____   8. _____

D Fill in the boxes with the correct spelling words.

1.    2.    3.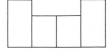

4.    5.   6.

Name _____

DAY 4

Homonyms

hare	**tail**	**sew**	**heal**
hair	**tale**	**sow**	**heel**

A **Use the correct spelling words to complete the story.**

Once upon a time there was a sly _____. This hare lived on a farm and loved it. He had a nice and cozy hole for a home. He had plenty of vegetables from the fields to eat. His favorite hobby was to play games and make the farmer mad.

One day the farmer spied the hare in the carrot patch. He crept toward the hare and reached out to grab the hare's _____. But the hare hopped away. This made the farmer so mad that he chased the hare across the field. The farmer tripped and fell, tearing his shirt. "You pesky hare!" cried the farmer. "Now I'll have to _____ my shirt back together." But the hare didn't hear the farmer. He was safely back in his hole.

B **Use each spelling word in a sentence.**

hare _____

hair _____

tail _____

tale _____

sew _____

sow _____

heal _____

heel _____

DAY
1

Words with -ves

leaves	knives	shelves	loaves
wolves	calves	thieves	lives

A Fill in each blank with a spelling word.

1. The cowboys caught the horse _____.

2. Can you help me put the books on the _____?

3. All the _____ in our kitchen are very sharp.

4. Three of our cows had _____.

5. How many _____ of bread did you buy at the store?

6. When fall comes, the _____ always pile up in the yard.

7. Many _____ were saved by the firefighters.

8. _____ are not mean animals as some people think.

B Circle the letters that are the same in all the spelling words.

leaves   wolves   knives   calves   shelves   thieves   loaves   lives

C Write the singular form of the spelling words.

1. _____ 2. _____ 3. _____ 4. _____

5. _____ 6. _____ 7. _____ 8. _____

D Find the missing letters. Then write the word.

1. ___ o l ___ ___ ___   _____

2. ___ e ___ ___ e s   _____

3. ___ ___ i e ___ ___ ___   _____

4. l ___ ___ ___ ___   _____

Name _____

Words with -*ves*

leaves	knives	shelves	loaves
wolves	calves	thieves	lives

A Use the correct spelling words to complete the story.

Someone who _____ his or her home to find a new home is

called a settler. Many years ago, the _____ of most settlers were

hard. They had to build their own houses. They grew all their own food.

They also had to protect themselves from _____ and bandits.

Sometimes they even had to fight off bears and _____.

B Write a spelling word under each picture.

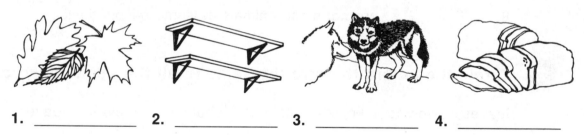

1. _____ 2. _____ 3. _____ 4. _____

C One word is wrong in each sentence. Circle the wrong word.
Then fill in the blank with a spelling word that makes sense.

1. We have to rake snow in the fall. _____

2. Please put the books on the top lamps. _____

3. We set the table with forks and hammers. _____

4. We bought ten quarts of bread for the picnic. _____

5. The scouts robbed the bank. _____

6. The firefighters saved many flowers in the rescue. _____

Words with -ves

leaves	knives	shelves	loaves
wolves	calves	thieves	lives

A **Find each hidden word from the list.**

leaves	calves	loaves	know
wolves	shelves	lives	pole
knives	thieves	home	stone

```
h  e  y  d  i  d  l  d  l  e  c  d  i  d  l  d  l
e  t  h  s  e  c  e  a  t  a  a  n  d  p  o  l  e
t  w  h  h  e  f  a  i  d  d  l  e  t  h  a  e  c
h  o  m  e  o  w  v  j  u  m  v  p  e  d  v  o  v
e  l  r  l  t  h  e  m  k  o  e  k  o  n  e  t  h
e  v  l  v  i  t  s  t  n  l  s  n  e  d  s  o  g
l  e  a  e  u  g  h  e  o  d  l  i  v  e  s  t  o
s  s  e  s  e  s  u  c  w  h  s  v  p  o  r  t  a
n  d  t  h  i  e  v  e  s  t  h  e  d  i  s  h  r
a  n  a  w  a  y  w  i  t  h  t  s  t  o  n  e  h
```

B **Match each spelling word with a related word.**

_____	**1.** leaves	**a.** barn
_____	**2.** wolves	**b.** rake
_____	**3.** knives	**c.** steal
_____	**4.** calves	**d.** bread
_____	**5.** shelves	**e.** pack
_____	**6.** thieves	**f.** cut
_____	**7.** loaves	**g.** books
_____	**8.** lives	**h.** births

Name _____

Lesson 25

DAY 4

Words with -ves

leaves	knives	shelves	loaves
wolves	calves	thieves	lives

A Fill in the boxes with the correct spelling words.

1.

2.

3.

4.

5.

6.

B Answer the questions with spelling words.

1. Which words have the long *e* sound?

_____   _____

2. Which word has five consonants? _____

3. Which words have the letter *o* in them?

_____   _____

C Use spelling words to complete the puzzle.

Across

2. They hold books.

4. wild animals

Down

1. robbers

3. Bread comes in ___.

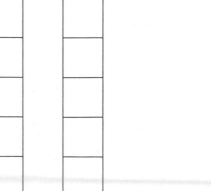

boxes	taxes	branches	churches	pennies
foxes	axes	speeches	catches	babies
fixes	mixes	stitches	crutches	cherries
waxes	sixes	scratches	matches	berries

A Write a spelling word under each picture.

1. _____ 2. _____ 3. _____

B Fill in each blank with a spelling word.

1. How many cake _____ did you buy?

2. I played two _____ of tennis with my friend.

3. If you break a leg, you may need _____ to walk.

4. You'll get _____ on your legs if you walk through the bushes.

5. You may need to give _____ if you are a leader of a club.

6. I had to pay _____ on those packages.

7. How many _____ of candy do you have?

8. The cut on his hand will need _____.

9. We saw one deer and three _____ in the woods.

10. My big brother always cleans and _____ his new car.

11. They attend both of those _____.

12. I put four _____ on my hot fudge sundae.

Name _____

ponies	hare	sew	leaves	shelves
puppies	hair	sow	wolves	thieves
cities	tail	heal	knives	loaves
guppies	tale	heel	calves	lives

C Write the spelling words that rhyme with the word pair.

1. hives   knives   _____

2. fives   lives   _____

3. halves   salves   _____

4. mow   low   _____

5. dare   rare   _____

6. sail   pail   _____

D Use the correct spelling words to complete the story.

My little sister's favorite thing to do is to visit pet stores. I usually take her to

a pet store at least once a month. She loves to look at all the animals in their

cages on the _____. After she finishes looking at the animals, she

always asks if she can hold the kittens and the _____. Sometimes I

even buy her something from the store.

One time my sister saw some brightly colored _____ swimming

around in a fish tank. She just had to have them! Now they are in a fish tank at

our house. My little sister takes very good care of them. Luckily she only wants

to keep tame animals as pets. She has never asked to keep _____

or bears at our house.

Words with -*sses*

dresses	illnesses	glasses	kisses
bosses	classes	guesses	losses

A Fill in each blank with a spelling word.

1. Doctors learn how to treat many _____.

2. At school I attend art and reading _____.

3. I broke my _____ and can't see very well.

4. He works for two _____ at his job.

5. Her closet is full of new _____.

6. Some people greet each other with _____ on the cheek.

7. The man at the carnival _____ your age.

8. The team had many wins and few _____.

B Circle the letters that are the same in all the spelling words.

dresses   bosses   illnesses   classes   glasses   guesses   kisses   losses

C Write the singular form of the spelling words.

1. _____   2. _____   3. _____   4. _____

5. _____   6. _____   7. _____   8. _____

D Fill in the boxes with the correct spelling words.

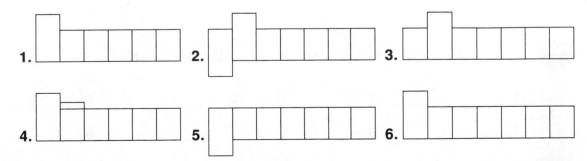

Name _____

Lesson 26

Words with -sses

dresses	illnesses	glasses	kisses
bosses	classes	guesses	losses

A **Use the correct spelling words to complete the story.**

When I was fifteen, we moved from Texas to New York. I was scared my first day of school there. It felt funny not knowing anyone. But the kids in all my _____ were nice. They asked me where I was from. I told them, "I'll give you three _____."

Everyone _____ the same in New York as in Texas. They like the same music and play the same sports. I played on a great baseball team in New York. We had almost no _____.

When we moved back to Texas, I left behind many good friends in New York. I hope to go back there again one day.

B **Write a spelling word under each picture.**

1. _____ 2. _____ 3. _____ 4. _____

C **Write the spelling words in alphabetical order.**

1. _____ 2. _____ 3. _____ 4. _____

5. _____ 6. _____ 7. _____ 8. _____

114

Words with -*sses*

dresses	illnesses	glasses	kisses
bosses	classes	guesses	losses

A Put an *X* on the word that is **not** the same.

1. dresses	dresses	dresses	dresses	tresses
2. bosses	bosses	bosses	dosses	bosses
3. illnesses	illmesses	illnesses	illnesses	illnesses
4. classes	classes	classes	closses	classes
5. glasses	glasses	glasses	glasses	glases
6. guesses	guesses	geusses	guesses	guesses

B Match each spelling word with the right clue.

_____   **1.** puts on clothes

_____   **2.** leaders or chiefs

_____   **3.** containers for drinks

_____   **4.** sicknesses

_____   **5.** things that are lost

_____   **6.** belongs with hugs

_____   **7.** what someone does when they don't know
the answer

_____   **8.** places where you learn

C Find the missing letters. Then write the word.

1. g l ____ ____ ___ e s   _____

2. l ____ s s ____ ____   _____

Name _____

DAY 4

Words with -sses

dresses   illnesses   glasses   kisses

bosses   classes   guesses   losses

A Use spelling words to complete the puzzle.

Across

4. sicknesses

5. gets dressed

6. chiefs

Down

1. You get three ___.

2. hugs and ___

3. They help you see better.

B Use each spelling word in a sentence.

dresses   _____

bosses   _____

illnesses   _____

classes   _____

glasses   _____

guesses   _____

kisses   _____

losses   _____

Irregular plural words

| men | children | mice | sheep |
| women | teeth | oxen | geese |

A **Fill in each blank with a spelling word.**

1. Cats love to chase _____.

2. Some farmers use _____ to pull their plows.

3. My dentist says my _____ are healthy and clean.

4. _____ fly in flocks and make honking sounds.

5. The wool for my sweater comes from _____.

6. Some games and toys aren't just for _____.

7. Boys grow up to become _____.

8. Girls grow up to become _____.

B **Write the singular form of the spelling words. Use a dictionary for help.**

Plural	Singular		Plural	Singular
1. men	_____		5. mice	_____
2. women	_____		6. oxen	_____
3. children	_____		7. sheep	_____
4. teeth	_____		8. geese	_____

C **Write the spelling words in alphabetical order.**

1. _____ 2. _____ 3. _____ 4. _____

5. _____ 6. _____ 7. _____ 8. _____

Name _____

Irregular plural words

men	children	mice	sheep
women	teeth	oxen	geese

A Write the spelling word that rhymes with the word pair.

1. hen   ten   _____

2. deep   keep   _____

3. dice   rice   _____

4. piece   lease   _____

B Write a spelling word under each picture.

1. _____   2. _____   3. _____   4. _____

C Use the correct spelling words to complete the story.

My friend is a special kind of doctor. She doesn't take care of grown-ups

and _____. She treats their pets.

Most of the time she cares for dogs, cats, birds, hamsters, and even

_____. She gives them their shots, makes them well when they're

sick, and cleans their _____.

Her partner works with large animals that live on farms. He sees horses,

cattle, and even ducks and _____.

I like to visit their office. One time a man came in with a pet raccoon.

Another time someone brought in a pet snake.

DAY 3

Irregular plural words

men	children	mice	sheep
women	teeth	oxen	geese

A **Find each hidden word from the list.**

men	teeth	sheep	rose
women	mice	geese	note
children	oxen	slope	drove

```
l  s  h  e  e  p  o  n  d  o  n  b  w  r  i  d  g
e  i  s  f  a  l  l  i  n  g  d  o  o  x  e  n  w
n  g  f  r  o  s  e  a  l  l  i  n  m  e  n  g  d
o  e  w  n  l  o  n  d  s  o  n  t  e  b  r  i  d
g  e  i  s  f  c  h  i  l  d  r  e  n  a  l  l  i
n  s  g  d  o  w  n  m  o  y  f  e  a  i  r  l  a
d  e  y  n  b  u  i  l  p  d  i  t  u  p  w  i  t
h  d  r  o  v  e  w  o  e  o  d  h  a  n  d  c  l
a  y  w  t  o  o  d  a  n  d  c  l  a  y  b  u  i
l  d  i  e  t  u  p  m  i  c  e  w  i  t  h  w  e
```

B **Match each spelling word with a related word.**

_____ **1.** men	**a.** cats	
_____ **2.** women	**b.** wool	
_____ **3.** children	**c.** kindergarten	
_____ **4.** teeth	**d.** plows	
_____ **5.** mice	**e.** boys	
_____ **6.** oxen	**f.** "honk"	
_____ **7.** sheep	**g.** girls	
_____ **8.** geese	**h.** mouth	

Name _____

Irregular plural words

men	children	mice	sheep
women	teeth	oxen	geese

A Fill in the boxes with the correct spelling words.

1.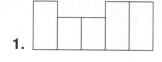

2.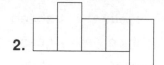

3.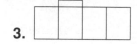

4.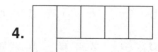

5.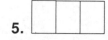

6.

B Answer each question with a spelling word.

1. Which word has the most letters? _____

2. Which word has three *e*'s? _____

3. Which is the shortest word? _____

C Use spelling words to complete the puzzle.

Across

4. more than one goose

5. more than one sheep

6. more than one woman

Down

1. more than one tooth

2. more than one man

3. more than one child

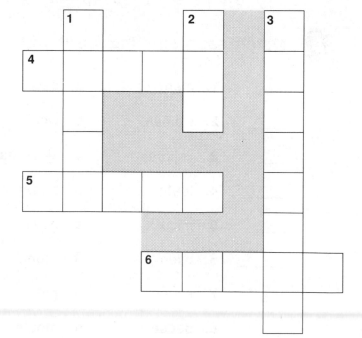

120

Lesson 28   Homonyms

know	write	hour	son
no	right	our	sun

A Fill in each blank with a spelling word.

1. Will you _____ to me while you're on your trip?

2. We're proud of _____ new car.

3. My sister's _____ is my nephew.

4. Do you _____ how to count change?

5. It takes an _____ to ride the bus home from work.

6. My friend said, "Take a _____ turn at the corner."

7. I have _____ idea how my pet snake escaped.

8. The _____ is our brightest star.

B Circle the correct answer to complete the sentence.

1. "Write" and "right" sound alike, but they _____.

    mean the same   are not spelled the same   look the same

2. The words in this lesson are _____.

    antonyms   homonyms   synonyms

C Find the missing letters. Then write the word.

1. ___ o u ___   _____

2. ___ ___ o w   _____

D Write the spelling words in alphabetical order.

1. _____ 2. _____ 3. _____ 4. _____

5. _____ 6. _____ 7. _____ 8. _____

Name _____

Homonyms

know	write	hour	son
no	right	our	sun

A Write the spelling words that rhyme with the word pair.

1. ton   fun   _____

2. light   sight   _____

3. flour   tower   _____

B Put an *X* on the word that is <u>not</u> the same.

1. know	know	know	krow	know
2. no	on	no	no	no
3. write	write	wrife	write	write
4. right	right	righf	right	right
5. hour	hour	hour	hour	houn
6. our	our	our	oun	our

C Match each spelling word with a related word.

_____ **1.** son	**a.** moon
_____ **2.** sun	**b.** your
_____ **3.** hour	**c.** yes
_____ **4.** our	**d.** pencil
_____ **5.** right	**e.** daughter
_____ **6.** write	**f.** minute
_____ **7.** know	**g.** left
_____ **8.** no	**h.** understand

Lesson 28 — Homonyms

know	write	hour	son
no	right	our	sun

A Use the correct spelling words to complete the story.

My teacher asked each person in my class to _____ a poem. The poem could be about anything we wanted. But I did not _____ what I wanted to write about. I needed to think about it for a while.

When I went home, I sat down to write my poem. I had so many ideas, but I couldn't decide which one to choose. "Maybe a walk will help me decide which idea I like the best," I said to myself. I walked for about an _____. Finally I thought of something to write about. My poem would be a beautiful story about the moon and the _____. I couldn't wait to go home and start writing!

B Write a spelling word under each picture.

1. _____   2. _____   3. _____   4. _____

C Write the spelling words that name things you <u>cannot</u> touch.

1. _____   2. _____   3. _____   4. _____

5. _____   6. _____   7. _____

Name _____

Homonyms

know	write	hour	son
no	right	our	sun

A Fill in the boxes with the correct spelling words.

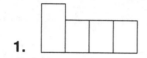

1.

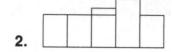

2.

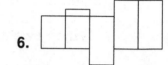

3.

4.

5.

6.

B Answer the questions with spelling words.

1. Which words begin with a silent letter?

   _____   _____   _____

2. Which words contain the letter *u*?

   _____   _____   _____

3. Which word contains a silent *gh*? _____

4. Which word is the shortest? _____

5. Which words contain the letter *i*? _____   _____

C Use each spelling word in a sentence.

know _____

no _____

write _____

right _____

hour _____

our _____

Lesson 29 — Compound words with *any-*

anyone	anybody	anyhow	anyway
anything	anyplace	anywhere	anytime

A **Fill in each blank with a spelling word.**

1. There are _____ from three to five opossums living under our house.

2. _____ you can do, I can do, too!

3. I don't know _____ by that name.

4. He can come to my house _____ he wants.

5. What do you want to do that for, _____?

6. You can put the box _____ you like.

7. Is there _____ here who can open this box?

8. I'm going _____, even if she's not.

B **Circle the letters that are the same in all the spelling words.**

anyone   anything   anybody   anyplace   anytime

C **Circle the correct answer to complete the sentence.**

1. All of the spelling words in this lesson are called _____.

   contractions   compacts   compounds

2. All of the spelling words have _____.

   one syllable   more than one syllable

D **Find the missing letters. Then write the word.**

1. a n y t ___ ___ ___   _____

2. a n y w ___ ___   _____

Name _____

125

DAY
2

Compound words with *any-*

anyone	anybody	anyhow	anyway
anything	anyplace	anywhere	anytime

A **Put an _X_ on the word that is <u>not</u> the same.**

1.	anyone	anyone	anynoe	anyone	anyone
2.	anything	anything	anything	anything	anythiny
3.	anybody	anybody	anyboby	anybody	anybody
4.	anyplace	anyglace	anyplace	anyplace	anyplace
5.	anyhow	anyhow	anyhow	anyhow	anybow
6.	anywhere	anywhere	anywheer	anywhere	anywhere
7.	anyway	anymay	anyway	anyway	anyway
8.	anytime	anytime	anyfime	anytime	anytime

B **Write the spelling words in alphabetical order.**

1. _____ 2. _____ 3. _____ 4. _____

5. _____ 6. _____ 7. _____ 8. _____

C **Use the correct spelling words to complete the story.**

There are times when I can't make up my mind. My friend called and

asked what I wanted to do tonight. "Oh, _____ is fine with me,"

I told him. He asked where I wanted to meet him. "_____ you

choose is all right," I said.

"What time shall we meet?" my friend asked.

"_____ that is good for you," I answered.

Compound words with *any-*

anyone	anybody	anyhow	anyway
anything	anyplace	anywhere	anytime

A **Find each hidden word from the list.**

anyone	anyplace	anyway	don't
anything	anyhow	anytime	fair
anybody	anywhere	own	chair

```
a  n  y  t  i  m  e  t  h  e  r  e  w  a  s  a  a
n  l  i  t  t  l  e  g  a  n  y  b  o  d  y  i  n
y  r  i  w  h  o  h  a  d  a  l  i  t  t  f  l  y
w  e  a  n  y  o  n  e  c  u  o  w  n  r  a  l  t
a  r  i  g  h  t  i  n  c  h  a  i  r  t  i  h  h
y  e  m  d  i  d  d  l  e  o  f  h  e  r  r  f  i
o  r  e  o  h  e  a  n  y  p  l  a  c  e  a  n  n
w  h  e  n  s  h  e  w  a  s  g  o  o  d  s  h  g
e  w  a  t  s  v  e  r  y  v  e  r  y  g  o  o  d
a  n  y  h  o  w  a  n  d  a  n  y  w  h  e  r  e
```

B **Fill in each blank with a spelling word.**

1. Write two words about people. _____   _____

2. Write two words about places. _____   _____

3. Write one word about time. _____

C **Match the spelling word with the word that is nearly the same.**

_____ 1. anybody   **a.** whenever

_____ 2. anytime   **b.** whatever

_____ 3. anything   **c.** whoever

Name _____

Lesson 29 Compound words with *any-*

anyone	anybody	anyhow	anyway
anything	anyplace	anywhere	anytime

A Make as many new words from each spelling word as you can.

1. anyone = *any*   *one*   *none*   *an*

2. anything = _____ _____ _____ _____

3. anybody = _____ _____ _____ _____

4. anyplace = _____ _____ _____ _____

5. anyhow = _____ _____ _____ _____

6. anywhere = _____ _____ _____ _____

7. anyway = _____ _____ _____ _____

8. anytime = _____ _____ _____ _____

B Use spelling words to complete the puzzle.

Across

2. Can ___ hear me?

3. Is there ___ I can do?

4. anyway

Down

1. anyhow

2. ___ can come to the party.

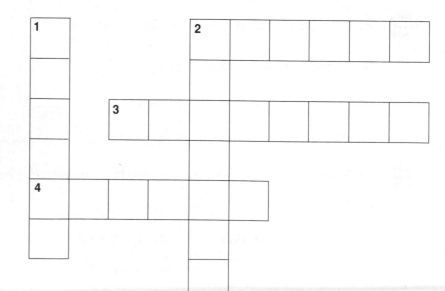

128

Compound words with *some-*

someone	somebody	somehow	sometime
something	someplace	somewhere	someday

A **Fill in each blank with a spelling word.**

1. _____ he was able to lift the car.

2. I would like to go to town _____ today.

3. This sunset is _____ to see!

4. I hope to visit Rome _____.

5. Let's go _____ and talk.

6. Can _____ help us?

7. _____ is looking for you over there.

8. I know that I put my socks _____, but I can't find them.

B **Circle the letters that are the same in all the spelling words.**

someone   something   somebody   someplace

somehow   somewhere   sometime   someday

C **Circle the correct answer to complete the sentence.**

1. All of the spelling words in this lesson are called _____.

    contractions   compounds   compacts

2. All of the spelling words have _____.

    one syllable   more than one syllable

D **Find the missing letters. Then write the word.**

s o m e h ___ ___   _____

Name _____

Lesson 30   Compound words with *some-*

someone	somebody	somehow	sometime
something	someplace	somewhere	someday

A   **Put an *X* on the word that is <u>not</u> the same.**

1. someone   someone   someoue   someone   someone

2. something   something   something   sowething   something

3. somebody   somedoby   somebody   somebody   somebody

4. someplace   someplace   someplace   someplace   someqlace

5. somehow   somebow   somehow   somehow   somehow

6. somewhere   somewhere   somewhere   somemhere   somewhere

7. sometime   sometime   sowetime   sometime   sometime

8. someday   someday   someday   someday   somebay

B   **Write the spelling words in alphabetical order.**

1. _____   2. _____   3. _____

4. _____   5. _____   6. _____

7. _____   8. _____

C   **Use the correct spelling words to complete the story.**

There are those in the world who are _____ able to write

great songs. One such song is "_____ Over the Rainbow."

Writing the words to a song is a lot like writing a poem. But then you

have to add music. It must be a hard thing to do. I think there's

_____ magic about how a song comes about. Maybe I'll write a

great song _____ .

Compound words with *some-*

someone	somebody	somehow	sometime
something	someplace	somewhere	someday

A Find each hidden word from the list.

someone	someplace	sometime	spare
something	somehow	someday	tear
somebody	somewhere	care	right

```
s  i  s  o  m  e  h  o  w  m  c  s  p  s  l  e  s  s
i  m  o  n  m  e  t  a  p  i  a  o  e  o  m  a  n  o
s  o  m  e  w  h  e  r  e  g  r  m  o  m  i  n  g  m
t  o  t  h  s  o  m  e  o  n  e  e  e  e  f  a  i  e
r  s  a  i  d  s  i  m  p  l  e  t  s  t  e  a  r  b
i  m  o  n  t  o  t  h  e  p  i  i  e  h  m  a  i  o
s  o  m  e  p  l  a  c  e  n  l  m  e  i  t  m  g  d
e  t  a  k  e  y  o  u  t  h  e  e  r  n  e  s  h  y
i  n  g  s  o  m  e  d  a  y  a  s  o  g  n  g  t  o
f  s  i  x  p  e  n  c  e  a  p  s  p  a  r  e  o  c
```

B Fill in each blank with a spelling word.

1. Write two words about people: _____ _____

2. Write two words about places: _____ _____

3. Write two words about time: _____ _____

C Write a spelling word that matches its opposite word.

1. never _____

2. nowhere _____

3. nobody _____

Name _____

Compound words with *some-*

someone	somebody	somehow	sometime
something	someplace	somewhere	someday

A Make as many new words from each spelling word as you can.

1. someone = *some*   *one*   *me*   *so*

2. something = _____ _____ _____ _____

3. somebody = _____ _____ _____ _____

4. someplace = _____ _____ _____ _____

5. somehow = _____ _____ _____ _____

6. somewhere = _____ _____ _____ _____

7. sometime = _____ _____ _____ _____

8. someday = _____ _____ _____ _____

B Use spelling words to complete the puzzle.

Across

1. on a later day

2. someplace

3. Is ___ wrong?

4. somewhere

Down

1. Come see me ___.

2. I'll find a way ___.

dresses	somehow	men	mice	know
bosses	anyhow	women	oxen	hour
illnesses	kisses	children	sheep	write
glasses	losses	teeth	geese	right

A Write a spelling word under each picture.

1. _____ 2. _____ 3. _____

B Fill in each blank with a spelling word.

1. We saw the _____ flying over our pond.

2. My grandparents always give me many hugs and _____.

3. I'm going to the dentist to have my _____ cleaned.

4. I studied hard, and I _____ the answers for the test.

5. The _____ were excited about their new toys.

6. Do you need to turn _____ or left at the light?

7. The _____ and women of our armed forces take care of

   our country.

8. You may need to wear _____ if you don't see well.

9. The baseball team had many wins and few _____.

10. My train leaves in one _____ and fifteen minutes.

11. Her sister bought two skirts and three _____.

Name _____

anyone	no	guesses	someone	anywhere
something	anything	classes	our	somewhere
somebody	anybody	anyway	son	sometime
someplace	anyplace	anytime	sun	someday

C **Write the spelling words that rhyme with the word pair.**

1. dresses   presses   _____

2. go   so   _____

3. passes   glasses   _____

4. run   bun   _____

D **Use the correct spelling words to complete the story.**

Has _____ ever told you _____ that was very hard to

believe? It happened to my family one time.

My younger brother told us that he had just seen _____ in the

woods wearing a big silver helmet. We thought he had made up the story, so

we told him to show us this person. He took us _____ in the woods

behind _____ house. We looked all around, but we didn't see

_____.

We waited a minute. Then we saw what he was talking about. The person

wearing the silver helmet was the tree trimmer for the electric power company!

Everyone in my family started laughing, and we gave my brother a big hug.

We felt much better. My little brother really had been telling the truth.

My Word List

Words I Can Spell

Put a ✓ in the box beside each word you spell correctly on your weekly test.

1

☐ her	☐ perch
☐ fern	☐ verb
☐ jerk	☐ herd
☐ nerve	☐ perk

2

☐ turn	☐ burst
☐ burn	☐ curve
☐ purse	☐ church
☐ nurse	☐ curb

3

☐ launch	☐ fault
☐ gauze	☐ cause
☐ vault	☐ haunt
☐ haul	☐ August

4

☐ red	☐ maid
☐ read	☐ made
☐ not	☐ be
☐ knot	☐ bee

5

☐ crawl	☐ fawn
☐ lawn	☐ claw
☐ dawn	☐ flaw
☐ yawn	☐ straw

Words To Review

If you miss a word on your test, write it here. Practice it until you can spell it correctly. Then check the box beside the word.

_____

_____

_____

_____

_____

_____

_____

_____

_____

_____

_____

_____

_____

_____

_____

_____

_____

Name _____

My Word List

Words I Can Spell

Put a ✓ in the box beside each word you spell correctly on your weekly test.

Words To Review

If you miss a word on your test, write it here. Practice it until you can spell it correctly. Then check the box beside the word.

6

☐ foot   ☐ stood
☐ hook   ☐ hood
☐ wood   ☐ crook
☐ brook   ☐ cook

7

☐ food   ☐ booth
☐ noon   ☐ tooth
☐ bloom   ☐ goose
☐ loose   ☐ proof

8

☐ thief   ☐ field
☐ chief   ☐ shield
☐ niece   ☐ brief
☐ piece   ☐ yield

9

☐ road   ☐ ate
☐ rode   ☐ eight
☐ pail   ☐ see
☐ pale   ☐ sea

10

☐ breath   ☐ feather
☐ spread   ☐ heavy
☐ thread   ☐ weather
☐ ready   ☐ leather

My Word List

Words I Can Spell

Put a ✓ in the box beside each word you spell correctly on your weekly test.

11

- ☐ heard
- ☐ learn
- ☐ earn
- ☐ pearl
- ☐ earth
- ☐ search
- ☐ yearn
- ☐ early

12

- ☐ cry
- ☐ fry
- ☐ dry
- ☐ shy
- ☐ fly
- ☐ sky
- ☐ spy
- ☐ pry

13

- ☐ to
- ☐ two
- ☐ for
- ☐ four
- ☐ bear
- ☐ bare
- ☐ flour
- ☐ flower

14

- ☐ sleigh
- ☐ freight
- ☐ weigh
- ☐ weight
- ☐ neighbor
- ☐ neigh
- ☐ eighty
- ☐ freighter

15

- ☐ kneel
- ☐ knock
- ☐ knife
- ☐ knit
- ☐ knot
- ☐ knob
- ☐ knight
- ☐ knack

Words To Review

If you miss a word on your test, write it here. Practice it until you can spell it correctly. Then check the box beside the word.

_____

_____

_____

_____

_____

_____

_____

_____

_____

_____

_____

_____

_____

_____

_____

_____

_____

Name _____

My Word List

Words I Can Spell

Put a ✓ in the box beside each word you spell correctly on your weekly test.

16

- ☐ wrench
- ☐ wring
- ☐ wrist
- ☐ wrong
- ☐ wreck
- ☐ wrestle
- ☐ wren
- ☐ wreath

17

- ☐ won't
- ☐ aren't
- ☐ isn't
- ☐ doesn't
- ☐ didn't
- ☐ wasn't
- ☐ hasn't
- ☐ weren't

18

- ☐ blew
- ☐ blue
- ☐ hear
- ☐ here
- ☐ sale
- ☐ sail
- ☐ knew
- ☐ new

19

- ☐ I'll
- ☐ you'll
- ☐ she'll
- ☐ he'll
- ☐ I've
- ☐ you've
- ☐ we've
- ☐ they've

20

- ☐ bushes
- ☐ wishes
- ☐ crushes
- ☐ flashes
- ☐ brushes
- ☐ dishes
- ☐ washes
- ☐ fishes

Words To Review

If you miss a word on your test, write it here. Practice it until you can spell it correctly. Then check the box beside the word.

_____

_____

_____

_____

_____

_____

_____

_____

_____

_____

_____

_____

_____

_____

_____

_____

_____

_____

My Word List

Words I Can Spell

Put a ✓ in the box beside each word you spell correctly on your weekly test.

21

- ☐ boxes
- ☐ foxes
- ☐ fixes
- ☐ waxes
- ☐ taxes
- ☐ axes
- ☐ mixes
- ☐ sixes

22

- ☐ branches
- ☐ speeches
- ☐ stitches
- ☐ scratches
- ☐ churches
- ☐ catches
- ☐ crutches
- ☐ matches

23

- ☐ pennies
- ☐ babies
- ☐ cherries
- ☐ berries
- ☐ ponies
- ☐ puppies
- ☐ cities
- ☐ guppies

24

- ☐ hare
- ☐ hair
- ☐ tail
- ☐ tale
- ☐ sew
- ☐ sow
- ☐ heal
- ☐ heel

25

- ☐ leaves
- ☐ wolves
- ☐ knives
- ☐ calves
- ☐ shelves
- ☐ thieves
- ☐ loaves
- ☐ lives

Words To Review

If you miss a word on your test, write it here. Practice it until you can spell it correctly. Then check the box beside the word.

_____

_____

_____

_____

_____

_____

_____

_____

_____

_____

_____

_____

_____

_____

_____

_____

_____

Name _____

My Word List

Words I Can Spell

Put a ✓ in the box beside each word you spell correctly on your weekly test.

26

- [ ] dresses
- [ ] bosses
- [ ] illnesses
- [ ] classes
- [ ] glasses
- [ ] guesses
- [ ] kisses
- [ ] losses

27

- [ ] men
- [ ] women
- [ ] children
- [ ] teeth
- [ ] mice
- [ ] oxen
- [ ] sheep
- [ ] geese

28

- [ ] know
- [ ] no
- [ ] write
- [ ] right
- [ ] hour
- [ ] our
- [ ] son
- [ ] sun

29

- [ ] anyone
- [ ] anything
- [ ] anybody
- [ ] anyplace
- [ ] anyhow
- [ ] anywhere
- [ ] anyway
- [ ] anytime

30

- [ ] someone
- [ ] something
- [ ] somebody
- [ ] someplace
- [ ] somehow
- [ ] somewhere
- [ ] sometime
- [ ] someday

Words To Review

If you miss a word on your test, write it here. Practice it until you can spell it correctly. Then check the box beside the word.

Name _____

Word Study Sheet

(Make a check mark after each step.)

Words	**1** Look at the Word	**2** Say the Word	**3** Think About Each Letter	**4** Spell the Word Aloud	**5** Write the Word	**6** Check the Spelling	**7** Repeat Steps (if needed)

Graph Your Progress

(Color or shade in the boxes.)

Number of words correctly spelled:

	Lesson 1	Lesson 2	Lesson 3	Lesson 4	Lesson 5	Lesson 6	Lesson 7	Lesson 8	Lesson 9	Lesson 10	Lesson 11	Lesson 12	Lesson 13	Lesson 14	Lesson 15	Lesson 16	Lesson 17	Lesson 18	Lesson 19	Lesson 20	Lesson 21	Lesson 22	Lesson 23	Lesson 24	Lesson 25	Lesson 26	Lesson 27	Lesson 28	Lesson 29	Lesson 30
8																														
7																														
6																														
5																														
4																														
3																														
2																														
1																														

Name